The **AA POCKET**Guide
VANCOUVER &
THE CANADIAN
ROCKIES

Vancouver & the Canadian Rockies: Regions and Best places to see

Written by Tim Jepson
Verified by Des Hannigan

© AA Media Limited 2010. First published 2009

ISBN: 978-0-7495-6416-2

Published by AA Publishing, a trading name of AA Media Limited, whose registered office is Fanum House, Basing View, Basingstoke, Hampshire RG21 4EA. Registered number 06112600.

Colour separation: MRM Graphics Ltd
Printed and bound in Italy by Printer Trento S.r.l.

Front cover images: (t) AA/C Sawyer; (b) AA/P Timmermans
Back cover image: AA/P Bennett

A04167
Mapping in this title produced from map data supplied by Global Mapping, Brackley, UK. Copyright © Global Mapping/ITMB

About this book

Symbols are used to denote the following categories:

➕ map reference

✉ address or location

☎ telephone number

🕐 opening times

💷 admission charge

🍴 restaurant or café on premises
  or nearby

Ⓔ nearest underground train station

🚌 nearest bus/tram route

🚉 nearest overground train station

⛴ nearest ferry stop

✈ nearest airport

❓ other practical information

ℹ tourist information

➤ indicates the page where you will
  find a fuller description

This book is divided into four sections.

Planning pages 6–19
Before you go; Getting there; Getting
around; Being there

Best places to see pages 20–41
The unmissable highlights of any visit
to Vancouver and the Canadian Rockies

Exploring pages 42–129
The best places to visit in Vancouver and
the Canadian Rockies, organized by area

Maps pages 133–144
All map references are to the atlas
section. For example, Calgary has the
reference ➕ 141 F8 – indicating the
page number and grid square in which it
is to be found

Contents

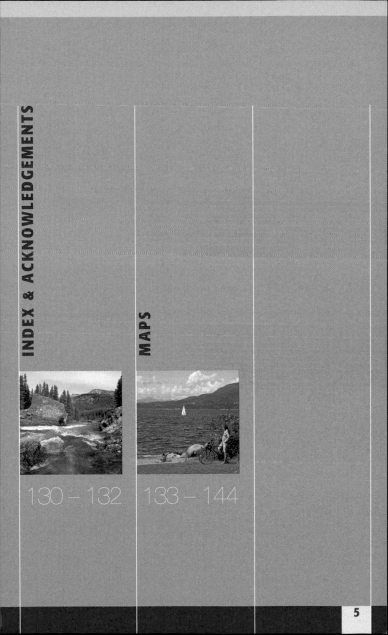

Planning

Before you go

WHEN TO GO

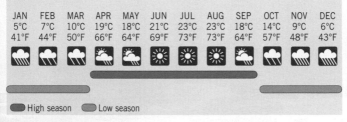

JAN	FEB	MAR	APR	MAY	JUN	JUL	AUG	SEP	OCT	NOV	DEC
5°C	7°C	10°C	19°C	18°C	21°C	23°C	23°C	18°C	14°C	9°C	6°C
41°F	44°F	50°F	66°F	64°F	69°F	73°F	73°F	64°F	57°F	48°F	43°F

🔵 High season ⚪ Low season

Temperatures are the average daily maximum for each month. The best time to visit Vancouver is June to August, when you can expect warm, sunny weather. The good weather often extends into September and October, when the city will also be less crowded and hotel prices lower. The same applies to much of interior British Columbia, though here conditions and temperatures can be more extreme and rainfall is generally lower. Snow is more prolonged, and cold more intense in mountainous areas, though the Okanagan region is an exception, with mild winters and hot, dry summers. In Calgary and the Rockies, snow can close roads for many months and persist on upland trails as late as June. Generally, July and August are warm fine months, and good, if popular, times to visit.

WHAT YOU NEED

● Required
○ Suggested
▲ Not required

Some countries require a passport to remain valid for a minimum period (usually at least six months) beyond the date of entry – check before you travel.

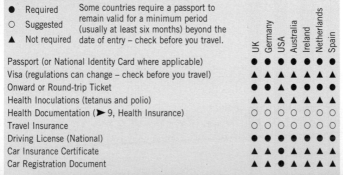

	UK	Germany	USA	Australia	Ireland	Netherlands	Spain
Passport (or National Identity Card where applicable)	●	●	●	●	●	●	●
Visa (regulations can change – check before you travel)	▲	▲	▲	▲	▲	▲	▲
Onward or Round-trip Ticket	●	●	▲	●	●	●	●
Health Inoculations (tetanus and polio)	▲	▲	▲	▲	▲	▲	▲
Health Documentation (➤ 9, Health Insurance)	○	○	○	○	○	○	○
Travel Insurance	○	○	○	○	○	○	○
Driving License (National)	●	●	●	●	●	●	●
Car Insurance Certificate	▲	▲	●	▲	▲	▲	▲
Car Registration Document	▲	▲	●	▲	▲	▲	▲

WEBSITES

www.tourismvancouver.com
www.tourismvictoria.com
www.hellobc.com

www.travelalberta.com
www.pc.gc.ca (National Parks)
www.canada.com

TOURIST OFFICES AT HOME

In the UK
PO Box 101, Chard,
Somerset, TA20 9AR
☎ 0870 380 0070
www.canada.travel

In the USA
www.canada.travel
(There is no phone or postal
contact/office for the general
public.)

HEALTH INSURANCE

Canada has excellent health provisions, but foreign visitors are required
to pay for treatment, so it is essential that you take out health and travel
insurance that will cover all potential costs, including the price of an
emergency flight home. The EHIC (European Health Insurance Card) does
not cover EU nationals for treatment in Canada. Keep all bills and receipts
to make a claim.

Dental care is also excellent but costly, so include this in your
insurance. Most hotels can recommend a dentist, or try the tourist office
or Yellow Pages. Again, keep all documentation for your claim.

TIME DIFFERENCES

GMT	Vancouver	Germany	USA (NY)	Netherlands	Spain
12 noon	4AM	1PM	7AM	1PM	1PM

Vancouver and much of British Columbia are on Pacific Time, eight hours
behind GMT (GMT-8). Calgary, Alberta and part of southeast British
Columbia observe Mountain Standard Time (GMT-7). Daylight saving
applies between April and October.

NATIONAL HOLIDAYS

Jan 1 *New Year's Day*
3rd Mon of Feb *Family Day* (Alberta)
Mar/Apr *Good Friday and Easter Monday*
3rd Mon in May *Victoria Day*
Jul 1 *Canada Day*
1st Mon in Aug *BC Day* (British Columbia)
1st Mon in Aug *Heritage Day* (Alberta)
1st Mon in Sep *Labour Day*
2nd Mon in Oct *Thanksgiving*
Nov 11 *Remembrance Day*
Dec 25 *Christmas Day*
Dec 26 *Boxing Day*

Banks, schools and government offices close on public holidays and many visitor attractions and transportation services follow Sunday openings and timetables. Holidays falling on a weekend are usually taken on the following Monday.

WHAT'S ON WHEN

The venues and events listed here are liable to change from one year to the next, and in the case of major festivals there is often more than one venue. Dates also vary slightly from year to year.

January *Chinese New Year:* 15 days of festivities (precise dates vary each year) in Vancouver's Chinatown and elsewhere. *Banff and Lake Louise Festival:* ski races, ice-sculpture competitions and skating parties.

February *Boat Show:* western Canada's largest and oldest boat show is held in Vancouver's BC Stadium over five days at the start of the month.

May *Vancouver Marathon* (first Sun in month): Canada's largest marathon attracts more than 6,000 runners (www.bmovanmarathon.ca). *International Children's Festival* (end of

May–early Jun): a week of events in Vancouver's Vanier Park attracts 70,000 people (www.childrensfestival.com).

June *Banff Festival:* large festival of the visual and performing arts.
Bard on the Beach (Jun–Sep): Shakespeare plays performed in outdoor venues in Vancouver (www.bardonthebeach.org).
Jazz Festival (10 days at end of month): more than 800 jazz and blues musicians perform at 25 venues around Vancouver (www.coastaljazz.ca).

July *Calgary Stampede:* one of the world's biggest and best rodeos.
Canada Day (Jul 1): celebrations across the region.
Folk Festival (3rd weekend of month): 30,000 people on Vancouver's Jericho Beach Park watch more than 100 different performers.
Celebration of Light (dates vary): the world's largest fireworks competition attracts 500,000 people to Vancouver's English Bay over four nights.

August *Abbotsford Air Show:* one of the world's best air shows takes place 58km (36 miles) from Vancouver (www.abbotsfordairshow.com).
Pride Parade: colorful parade and events celebrating Vancouver's gay and lesbian community (www.vancouverpride.ca).

September *Fringe Theatre Festival* (10–14 days mid-month): theater, comedy and dance groups perform more than 500 shows at venues around Vancouver.
Vancouver Film Festival (17 days): North America's third-largest film festival presents more than 500 screenings of films new and old (www.viff.org).

October *Wine festivals:* events and tastings held across the Okanagan region to celebrate the wine harvest.

November *VanDusen Market and Festival of Light* (late Nov–Dec): gift and craft market in Vancouver's VanDusen garden, which is illuminated with 20,000 lights.

December *Christmas Carol Ship Parade* (3 weeks to Christmas): magical flotillas of illuminated boats with carol singers in Vancouver's harbor.

Getting there

BY AIR

Vancouver Airport

10km (6 miles) to city center

🚊 20 minutes

🚌 35–45 minutes

🚗 35–45 minutes

Calgary Airport

15km (9 miles) to city center

🚌 30 minutes

🚗 30 minutes

The main entry to Vancouver and western British Columbia is Vancouver International Airport (tel: 604/207-7077; www.yvr.ca). SkyTrain (tel: 604/953-3333; www.translink.bc.ca), the city's light-transit system (➤ 14), runs from the airport to Waterfront Station near Canada Place. Alternatively, take the Airporter shuttle bus (tel: 604/946-8866 or 1-800/668-3141; www.yvrairporter.com) from outside the International Arrivals terminal (every 20–30 minutes from 5:20am–11:45pm).

For Banff, Calgary and the Canadian Rockies, Calgary Airport (tel: 403/735-1200 or 1-877/254-7427; www.calgaryairport.com) is a more convenient entry point.

BY TRAIN

Vancouver is served by VIA Rail (tel: 1-888/842-7245; www.viarail.com) services from Kamloops, Jasper and points in eastern Canada, plus Amtrak (tel: 1-800/872-7245; www.amtrak.com) services from Eugene, Portland and Seattle. Trains arrive at the Pacific Central Station alongside the bus terminal (➤ 13). Calgary has no public train service, but is served by occasional expensive private charter trains.

BY CAR

From eastern Canada or central US, the main Trans-Canada Highway (Hwy 1) runs through the heart of British Columbia to Vancouver via

Calgary, Banff and Kamloops. Hwy 3 is a slower trans-provincial route in the south shadowing the US border; Hwy 6 is a still slower but scenic route through the center of the province. Hwy 5 and Hwy 16 form another scenic road, linking Vancouver and Jasper.

BY BUS

Greyhound (tel: 1-800/661-8747; www.greyhound.ca) offers a network of services across most of Canada, including several services daily between Calgary and Vancouver and many points in between, including Banff and Lake Louise. From Vancouver's main bus terminal (1150 Station Street) take a taxi to downtown for around $7–$10 or the SkyTrain service to Waterfront Station from Science World-Main Street station, 150m (165yds) from the terminal.

Getting around

PUBLIC TRANSPORTATION

Internal flights Air Canada (www.aircanada.ca), plus smaller regional airlines, including seaplane operators such as Harbour Air (tel: 604/274-1277; www.harbour-air.com) in Vancouver, provide regular services between Vancouver, Calgary, Victoria and Edmonton, plus the Gulf Islands and many other smaller centers in British Columbia.

Trains Railway services are limited. VIA Rail (tel: 1-888/842-7245; www.viarail.com) has three services weekly between Vancouver and eastern Canada via Kamloops, Jasper and Edmonton, plus services from Victoria to Courtenay on Vancouver Island and from Jasper to Prince George and Prince George to Prince Rupert.

Regional buses Greyhound (tel: 1-800/661-8747; www.greyhound.ca) provides the majority of regional bus services. Key smaller operators include Pacific Coach Lines (tel: 604/662-7575 or 1-800/661-1725; www.pacificcoach.com) for services from Vancouver to Victoria, inclusive of ferry crossing, and Perimeter (tel: 604/266-5386 or 1-877/317-7788; www.perimeterbus.com) for departures to Whistler.

Ferries Victoria has ferry connections to Seattle and to various other points on the US west coast. BC Ferries (tel: 250/386-3431; www.bcferries.com) offers ferries from Vancouver to Victoria and other towns on Vancouver Island, plus the Gulf Islands. It also runs ferries from Port Hardy on Vancouver Island to Prince Rupert. Vancouver is a major port for cruise ships.

Urban transportation Translink (tel: 604/953-3333; www.translink.bc.ca) operates Vancouver's public transportation (or transit) system, which includes buses, the SeaBus to North Vancouver, and SkyTrain, a light-rail network. Tickets and day passes should be bought before traveling at authorized outlets or ticket vending machines. The tickets are then valid across all three services for 90 minutes from the moment they are validated.

TAXIS

Vancouver taxis are inexpensive and efficient. If you can't find a cab
on the street, head for the big hotels, where taxis tend to congregate.
Alternatively, call a cab from Black Top & Checker (tel: 604/731-1111),
Maclure's (tel: 604/683-6666) or Vancouver Taxi (tel: 604/871-1111).

DRIVING

- In Canada, you drive on the right and pass on the left.
- All persons in a car must wear seat belts.
- Right turns are allowed at red lights, after coming to a full stop, unless
  otherwise indicated.
- Distances and speed limits are given in kilometers and kilometers per
  hour. Speed limits vary between provinces, but are generally 100kph
  (62mph) on expressways, 70–90kph (43–56mph) on other major roads,
  and 50kph (31mph) or less in urban areas.
- Fuel (gas) is sold by the liter. Fill up when you can in mountain areas,
  where fuel stops may be few and far between.
- Most roads are of high quality, but some mountain roads may be
  surfaced with gravel rather than asphalt.
- If you intend to drive long distances, consider joining the Canadian
  Automobile Association (www.caa.ca).
- In case of emergency, call 911.

CAR RENTAL

Car rental is available at airports, cities and resorts, as well as many
towns. Rates depend on location. You must be over 21 to rent a car, and
have ID and a valid driver's license, which you have held for at least a
year. If crossing between Alberta and British Columbia, check that the
rental agreement allows you to take the car into another province. Also
check for penalties when dropping a car in a different place to where it
was rented. If you rent in the US, carry a copy of the rental agreement.
Rental companies often do not allow cars to be taken on gravel roads.

FARES AND CONCESSIONS

Children and students in possession of valid student ID, plus seniors,
often qualify for reductions on public transportation and many attractions
in Vancouver and across British Columbia and the Canadian Rockies.

Being there

TOURIST OFFICES

- **Vancouver**
TouristInfo Centre, 200 Burrard Street ☎ 604/683-2000;
www.tourismvancouver.com

- **Victoria**
812 Wharf Street ☎ 250/953-2033; www.tourismvictoria.com

- **Banff**
224 Banff Avenue ☎ 403/762-1550; www.pc.gc.ca or www.banfflakelouise.com

- **Calgary**
Calgary Tower, 101 9th Avenue SW
☎ 403/750-2362;
www.tourismcalgary.com

- **Jasper**
500 Connaught Drive
☎ 780/852-6176; www.pc.gc.ca

- **Lake Louise**
Lake Louise Village
☎ 403/522-3833; www.pc.gc.ca
or www.banfflakelouise.com

MONEY

A Canadian dollar is made up of 100 cents. The one cent piece, or penny, is copper in color. There are also five-cent pieces (nickels), ten cents (dimes) and 25 cents (quarters). The gold-colored one-dollar piece is known as a "loonie." The two-dollar piece, or "toonie," is silver and gold. Notes (bills) come in denominations of $5 (blue), $10 (purple), $20 (green), $50 (pink) and $100 (brown). There have been counterfeit problems with $50 and $100 notes. New designs for $5, $10 and $20 notes have been introduced, but old designs remain legal tender.

All major credit cards are accepted and there are ATMs, banks and other exchange facilities. UK and European visitors should check with their bank about withdrawing cash from ATMs.

TIPS/GRATUITIES

Yes ✓ No ✗		
Hotels (if service included)	✓	change
Restaurants (if service not included)	✓	15–20%
Cafés/bars (if service not included)	✓	change
Taxis	✓	change
Tour guides	✓	$1
Porters/chambermaids	✓	$1
Toilet attendants	✗	

POSTAL AND INTERNET SERVICES

Stamps can be bought from post offices and outlets with post office facilities (look for blue-and-red window signs), notably convenience stores such as 7-Eleven and Shopper's Drug Mart. Vancouver's main post office is 349 West Georgia Street at Homer Street, tel: 604/662-5723; www.canadapost.ca, open Mon–Fri 8–5:30. There are plans under way to relocate it.

The internet is accessible across Canada, with many cybercafés in towns and cities and WiFi and broadband connections in many hotels. However, access is often restricted in mountain and other rural areas.

TELEPHONES

Emergency telephone numbers

Police, fire, ambulance and general emergencies ☎ 911

Outgoing calls

To call abroad the prefix is 011, then the country code: for the UK dial 011 44 then the number minus the "0" at the start of the area code. For Australia the country code is 61, New Zealand 64 and the Republic of Ireland 353.

Calls to the US

It is easy to make calls directly to the US from Canada. Dial 1 followed by the state or city code, then the telephone number.

Incoming calls

To call Vancouver from the UK and the rest of Europe, dial 001 and then the number, including the 604 prefix. The 604 prefix must always be dialed, even when calling 604 numbers within Vancouver itself.

Regional phone codes

The code for Victoria and most of interior British Columbia is 250. Calgary and parts of the Rockies have a 403 code. In Jasper and northern British Columbia the code is 867.

Calls from hotels

You often pay a high tariff to use direct-dial services from hotel rooms. However, many Vancouver hotels offer free local calls (604 numbers within the city).

Mobile (cell) phones

Contact your service provider to check whether your handset will work on Canada's 1900 megaHerz network.

Pay phones
Use 25¢ coins and/or credit cards. Dial "0" for an operator, "00" for the international operator. For directory enquiries, call 411: the cost is 75¢.

CUSTOMS REGULATIONS
Adults over 19 can bring 1.14L of wine or spirits, 8.5L of beer, 200 cigarettes, 50 cigars and 200g of tobacco into the country. Also allowed are gifts up to a value of $65 and a "reasonable" amount of goods such as computers and outdoor equipment for personal use. Firearms are prohibited, as are meat, fish, fruit, vegetables and plants. Contact the Canada Customs and Revenue Agency (tel: 204/983 3500 or 1-800/461-9999; www.ccra-adrc.gc.ca/visitors) for more information.

METRIC MEASUREMENTS
Canada uses the metric system of weights and measures: centimeters, meters and kilometers for distance, grams and kilograms for weight, liters for fuel.

OPENING HOURS

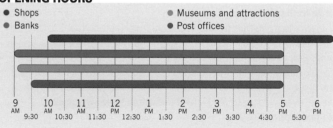

Shops: Vary considerably. Most city shops, especially those in busy or tourist areas, open daily in summer 10–8 or later; otherwise Mon–Sat 10–5. Convenience stores have longer hours, often 24 hours daily.
Banks: Most banks open Mon–Fri 9 or 9:30–5, though some may open from 8–8 plus shorter hours on Sat, but close Mon.
Museums and attractions: Vary considerably. Many have shorter hours from Labour Day (first Mon in Sep) to Victoria Day (third Mon in May).
Post offices: Generally Mon–Fri 9:30–5, sometimes Sat 10–4 or similar, but outlets in convenience stores have longer hours.

ELECTRICITY

Canada operates on 110V, 60-cycle electric power, like the US. UK and European appliances on 220/240V and 50 cycles may not function properly. Plugs are either two-pin (flat) or three-pin (two flat, one round). UK and European visitors will need an adaptor.

CONSULATES IN VANCOUVER

Australia: Suite 1225, 888 Dunsmuir Street at Hornby Street ☎ 604/684-1177
France: 1130 West Pender Street at Thurlow Street ☎ 604/681-4345
Germany: Suite 704, World Trade Centre, 999 Canada Place at Hornby Street ☎ 604/684-0377
New Zealand: Suite 1200, 888 Dunsmuir Street at Hornby Street ☎ 604/684-7388

Republic of Ireland: Suite 1000, 10th Floor, 100 West Pender Street at Abbott Street ☎ 604/683-9233
United Kingdom: Suite 800, 1111 Melville Street at Thurlow Street ☎ 604/683-4421
United States: 1075 West Pender Street at Thurlow Street ☎ 604/685-4311

HEALTH AND PERSONAL SAFETY

Canada is generally a safe country, but parts of Vancouver, notably on the fringes of Chinatown and the streets around Main and East Hastings between Gastown and Chinatown, should be avoided, especially after dark. In rural areas, the main health risks are biting insects (black flies, horseflies and mosquitoes).

When camping, be careful with water to avoid the giardia parasite, and consult visitor centers for advice on bear sightings if you are hiking in bear country. Poison ivy, which causes itchy open blisters and lumpy sores, is a consideration when outdoors: ointments are available from pharmacies. Also prevalent is lyme borreliosis ("lyme tick disease"), which causes a large rash and flu-like symptoms and can be very dangerous if left untreated. If in any doubt, consult a doctor.

There is no shortage of pharmacies (chemists) in Canadian cities, and some stay open for 24 hours. Carry a supply of any prescription you have to take as Canadian pharmacies will not accept an out-of-province presciption. You would have to visit a Canadian doctor and get a new prescription that's recognized locally.

Best places to see

1

Butchart Gardens

www.butchartgardens.com

The Butchart Gardens, north of Victoria on Vancouver Island, are some of the most striking and most visited gardens in Canada.

To look at the horticultural displays of the Butchart Gardens today, it's hard to imagine that they started life as a bleak and unprepossessing quarry. Founded in 1904, the gardens owe their existence to Jenny Butchart, wife of R.P. Butchart, a mining magnate who made a fortune by pioneering the use of Portland cement in Canada and the US.

The enterprising Jenny decided to landscape one of her husband's former quarries, little suspecting that her project would expand to include gardens that now attract more than half a million visitors annually and contain more than a million plants and 700 floral and arboreal species.

These species are planted in many specialist areas, such as rose, Italian and Japanese gardens, but also across wide areas as simple decorative features. Some visitors may find the site a little over-commercialized, with its large gift store, restaurant and car park, but it's easy to leave the bustle behind, especially out of peak season. This said, one of the garden's most popular attractions takes place in high summer, when the gardens

stay open late and spectacular fireworks displays are held, usually on Saturdays.

Note that if you are in Victoria for a couple of days without a car, it is possible to reach the gardens either on public transportation, as part of a tour, or by using a regular dedicated shuttle bus from the city's main bus terminal.

✚ 134 F1 ✉ 800 Benvenuto Avenue, Brentwood Bay, 23km (14 miles) north of Victoria ☎ 250/652-4422 or 1-866/652-4422 ⊙ Mid-Jun to Aug daily 9am–10pm; first 2 weeks of Sep, Dec daily 9–9; rest of the year daily 9am–sunset ✋ Very expensive (reductions in low season) 🍴 Café and restaurant on site 🚌 75 ❓ Tickets can be purchased online

2 Canada Place

www.canadaplace.ca
www.portvancouver.com

Canada Place is a major landmark on Vancouver's waterfront, its combination of superb views and interpretive walkways offering a perfect introduction to the city.

Canada Place was built as the Canadian Pavilion for Expo '86, a vast world trade and exposition fair held in 1986. The event helped mark Vancouver's centennial and, for the first time, brought the city to wider international prominence. Seen from afar, the former pavilion is designed to look like a ship, notably in the shape of its vast, white Teflon roof, which resembles sails – a deliberate homage to the importance of Vancouver's port and maritime past.

The Expo event, and Canada Place in particular, began an extensive period of city redevelopment, much of which continues to this day. No longer a simple exhibition space, the complex now contains a convention center, the luxury Pan Pacific hotel, a port interpretive center, and a large-screen IMAX cinema.

For most visitors, however, the building's appeal focuses on the walkways around the perimeter, which offer magnificent views of the port, Stanley Park to the west, and the mountains above North Vancouver, across the Burrard Inlet. These walkways include the "Promenade into History," 44 illustrated infoboards devoted to episodes from the city's past and aspects of the surrounding view. The combination of a central position, the magnificent vistas and the easily absorbed nuggets of history make this the perfect place to visit on your first day in Vancouver.

✚ 142 C3 ✉ 999 Canada Place Way, Vancouver
☎ Canada Place 604/647-7390. IMAX Theatre 604/682-IMAX; www.imax.com/vancouver ⏰ Walkways: 24 hours. Interpretive Centre Mon–Fri 8–5 ✋ Walkways free, IMAX Theatre expensive 🍴 Food outlets in convention center 🚇 Waterfront 🚌 6, 44, 50 ❓ Vancouver's main visitor center (➤ 16) is opposite Canada Place

3 Granville Island

www.granvilleisland.com

One of Vancouver's most tempting attractions combines shops, galleries, cafés, restaurants, people-watching and one of North America's finest markets.

Granville Island is a delightful place, a city regeneration project that succeeded beyond its planners' wildest dreams. For years it was little more than a swamp, tucked away on False Creek, the arm of water that marks the southern limit of Vancouver's downtown peninsula. In 1916 it was drained, and became a flourishing site for a wide range of light industry. Over the years, though, fire and other mishaps laid it low, and by the 1970s it had become a rubbish-strewn wasteland.

The transformation since the late 1970s has cleverly encouraged new light-industrial initiatives, together with a major art school and artisans' workshops, adding a welcome, gritty edge to what might otherwise have become a twee, tourist-oriented venture.

At the island's heart is a covered market, teeming with superlative meat, fruit, fish and vegetable stalls, and all manner of cafés and gourmet and specialist stores. You can also visit the **Granville Island Brewery** and a trio of **museums** devoted to fishing and model ships and railways; ride a converted

streetcar; see a show at the Arts Club; or dine at one of the many informal restaurants.

Come by bus or taxi (it is not a nice walk from downtown), or board one of the ferries that ply False Creek and that also run to Science World (➤ 64) and Vanier Park's museums (➤ 68–69).

✚ 142 D2 ✉ Visitor center, 1661 Duranleau Street, Vancouver ☎ 604/666-5784. Public market 604/666-6477 🕐 Market daily 9–7 🍴 Many cafés, restaurants and food stalls 🚌 50 🚢 Aquabus and False Creek services

Granville Island Brewery

✉ 1441 Cartwright Street ☎ 604/687-2739; www.gib.ca 🕐 3 tours daily: times vary 🖐 Moderate

Museums

✉ 1502 Duranleau Street ☎ 604/683-1939; www.modeltrainsmuseum.ca, www.trams.bc.ca, www.modelshipsmuseum.ca 🕐 Tue–Sun 10–5:30 🖐 Combined ticket moderate

4 Grouse Mountain

www.grousemountain.com

Climb aboard North America's largest cable car for a ride up Grouse Mountain, a natural vantage point that offers magnificent views of Vancouver and its hinterland.

One of Vancouver's great charms is the proximity of glorious scenery to the city center, not least Grouse Mountain (1,250m/4,100ft), which is one of the forest-covered peaks you see as you gaze north from the downtown district, across the waters of the Burrard Inlet. Jump aboard the SeaBus ferry (▶ 58), or board a bus or taxi at Lonsdale Quay at the ferry's terminus, and in a few minutes you are at the base station of the so-called Skyride, the twin, Swiss-built cable cars (they are North America's largest) that carry well over a million visitors a year up Grouse Mountain. It is well worth arriving as early as possible to avoid waiting in line.

At the top of the ride is the Alpine Station, which contains an informal café-bistro and a more formal restaurant, plus a theater where you can watch free film presentations on the mountain and British Columbia in general. Beyond here, you can walk the much-tramped upland meadows, where other attractions include wolf and bear enclosures and regular falconry displays and lumberjack shows. You can also walk short trails (longer hikes are possible), but when all's said and done, the highlights here are the sublime views, which on clear days extend for 113km (70 miles) or more to Vancouver Island and Washington State in the US.

🔲 144 A6 ✉ 6400 Nancy
Greene Way, North Vancouver
☎ 604/980-9311 or 604/980-0661
🕐 Skyride daily every 15 mins
9am–10pm 💵 Expensive
🍴 Altitudes Bistro ($) and Observ-
atory Restaurant ($$) in Alpine
Centre. Starbucks ($) at Skyride base
station 🚢 SeaBus ferry to Lonsdale
Quay, then bus 236 ❓ Reservations
at Alpine Centre's Observatory Rest-
aurant include the price of Skyride

5 Icefields Parkway

www.columbiaicefield.com

It's hard to imagine a more scenic drive than the Icefields Parkway, a panoramic road that runs through the majestic heart of the Canadian Rockies.

The Icefields Parkway stretches for 230km (143 miles) from Lake Louise (➤ 122–123) in Banff National Park almost to the town of Jasper in Jasper National Park (➤ 116–117). En route it passes an unending succession of peaks,

glaciers, lakes and upland meadows, with innumerable opportunities to stop at viewpoints or to follow short trails (although many much longer hikes are also possible). The drive's high point is the Columbia Icefield, the largest glacial area in the northern hemisphere outside the Arctic Circle. Here you can admire the glaciers from afar or board an "Ice Explorer" vehicle from the roadside Icefield Centre. This is one of only two major stops for fuel and food on the highway, the other being Saskatchewan Crossing, 77km (48 miles) from Lake Louise.

Ideally, you should allow a day for the journey, which will give you time to pause and take the odd walk. Although there is virtually no development en route, the road's points of interest are well signed. Early highlights include Bow Lake and Bow Glacier Falls and their respective trails, close to the Num-Ti-Jah Lodge, where you can stop for coffee (or stay overnight). The best viewpoint is Peyto Lake, reached via a short trail. Parker Ridge is another good, short trail, as is Wilcox Pass. Jasper or Lake Louise visitor centers carry full details of all the trails and other highlights.

✚ 140 C4 ✉ Icefield Centre ☎ 780/852-6288 🕓 May to mid-Jun, Sep to mid-Oct daily 9–5; mid-Jun to Aug daily 9–6. Closed rest of the year ✋ Ice Explorer tours, very expensive 🍴 Num-Ti-Jah Lodge ($), Saskatchewan Crossing, Icefield Centre 🚌 Mid-May to mid-Oct daily Brewster bus service Banff–Jasper

6 Kootenays

www.kaslo.com
www.newdenver.ca
www.nakusphotsprings.com
www.discovernelson.com

The Kootenays is a peaceful enclave of lakes and mountains in southeast British Columbia, full of quaint villages, pretty drives and superlative scenery.

Few regions, even in British Columbia, offer as many scenic rewards as the Kootenays, which consists of two large north–south valleys, the Columbia and the Kootenay. These valleys are largely taken up with Kootenay Lake and the Upper and Lower Arrow Lakes, plus the intervening mountain ranges – the Purcells, Selkirks and Monashees.

Although the lakes and the arrangement of mountain roads preclude an obvious round-trip in the region, you could easily spend a week or more driving the area's many panoramic roads, exploring the rich mining heritage, or taking time in some of the many attractive villages. As ever, in British Columbia, there are also countless hiking and other outdoor activities.

The prettiest village is lakeside Kaslo, followed closely by New Denver and Nakusp (which has natural hot springs), but it is well worth allowing for an overnight stop in Nelson (► 96–97), the region's main town. A good base, Nelson is also an attractive town in its own right, full of old wooden heritage buildings and many galleries and specialist stores. The region's most scenic drives are Nakusp-New Denver-Kaslo, followed by Needles to Coldstream (and onward to the Okanagan, ➤ 101) and the lakeside roads from Creston-Balfour-Kaslo and Needles-Nakusp-Galena Bay.

✚ 137 E7

🛈 324 Front Street, Kaslo ☎ 250/353-2525

🛈 202 6th Avenue, New Denver ☎ 250/358-2719

🛈 225 Hall Street, Nelson ☎ 250/352-3433

🛈 92 West Street and 2nd Avenue, Nakusp
☎ 250/265-4234

7 Moraine Lake

www.pc.gc.ca

Even in the Canadian Rockies, a region of sublime landscapes, Moraine Lake stands out, a perfect ensemble of water, forest and mountain.

Moraine Lake is just 13km (8 miles) from Lake Louise (➤ 122–123), in Banff National Park. It is smaller and marginally less-visited than its more famous neighbor, but in many ways it is scenically superior. At the right time of the year, when glacial till, or silt, fills the lake, the shimmering water is a sublime turquoise, the perfect complement to the jagged and snow-covered peaks of the Wenkchemna mountains. Almost nothing disturbs this faultless scene, save for the visitors and the well-designed Moraine Lake Lodge on the lake edge, where you can stay or buy coffee and snacks or fuller meals.

   At busy times, the approach road is crowded, and the park authorities run a shuttle bus from Lake Louise to reduce the volume of traffic. But even large numbers of visitors cannot detract from the lake's beauty, which you can savor by following the easy trail along its northern shore or by renting a canoe from the lodge. You can also clamber over the massive rock fall that created the lake (not a glacial moraine, despite the name), or follow the

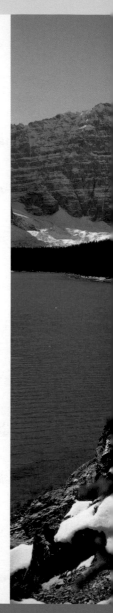

longer (but still easy) one-hour trail to Consolation Lake. More demanding hikes climb to Larch Valley-Sentinel Pass and Eiffel Lake-Wenkchemna Pass: full details are available from the Lake Louise park visitor center.

➕ 141 E5 🍴 Moraine Lake Lodge ($–$$$) 🚌 Greyhound and Brewster services to Lake Louise Village; shuttle bus from Lake Louise

ℹ️ Lake Louise Village

☎ 403/522-3833

8 Museum of Anthropology

www.moa.ubc.ca

Vancouver's most dazzling museum is devoted to the totems, monumental art, jewelry and other artifacts of western Canada's First Nations peoples.

The original inhabitants of Canada's west coast and northern extremes – notably the Inuit and Haida – were some of the most sophisticated of all First Nations peoples, and produced (and continue to produce) exceptional works of art – anything from the tiniest bone carving and amber beads to vast wooden sculptures and colossal totem poles. Some of the best examples of their work over many centuries have been collected in this

museum, housed in a superb modern building on the University of British Columbia (UBC) campus, designed by the celebrated local architect, Arthur Erickson.

The museum is 20 minutes' drive or bus ride from the city center, but is well worth the trip, which can be extended to include the Nitobe Memorial Garden and UBC Botanical Garden (➤ 62). The building's star turn is the Great Hall, a vast, light-filled gallery built to accommodate the totems and other large-scale works of art. Compare the traditional artifacts here with *The Raven and the*

First Men, a monumental sculpture by the modern Haida artist, Bill Reid (1920–98).

Other highlights include the art- and artifact-filled drawers of the Visible Storage Gallery, designed

to allow as much of the museum's vast collection as possible to be displayed. Other parts of the museum are devoted to art from other aboriginal peoples around the world, while outside you can walk around a fascinating reconstructed First Nations village.

✚ 142 E1 ✉ 6393 NW Marine Drive, Vancouver ☎ 604/822-3825 or 604/822-5087 🕓 Mid-May to mid-Oct daily 10–5 (also Tue 5–9); mid-Oct to mid-May Wed–Sun 11–5 (also Tue 5–9) ✋ Moderate. By donation Tue 5–9 🍴 Café on site 🚌 4, 17, 44 to UBC, then 10-min walk

9 Royal BC Museum

www.royalbcmuseum.bc.ca

This magnificent museum offers a fascinating survey of British Columbia's rich past, natural history and First Nations peoples.

Visitor and magazine surveys often rate Victoria's Royal BC Museum as one of the best in North America, and it's easy to see why. Every aspect of the province is explored, but the displays are a world away from the dusty exhibits of yesteryear. The dazzling, contemporary approach is most obvious in the natural history section, where a series of mind-boggling displays reproduce many of British Columbia's natural habitats. Every detail is covered, right down to the dripping water and cool, dank atmosphere of a marsh on the Fraser delta, or the birdsong and haunting animal cries of the region's temperate rain forests.

Many museums in towns and cities in British Columbia, including the Vancouver Museum (➤ 68–69), aim to evoke the region's First Nations and pioneer past, but none do it as well as here. Part of an early 20th-century frontier village is re-created, along with exhibits that fully explain vital aspects of the province's past, notably forestry, fishing, farming, silver mining and the gold rush. Vancouver's Museum of Anthropology (➤ 36–37) may feature the best of the region's First Nations art, but this museum presents the definitive account of the often tragic history of British Columbia's original

inhabitants, both before and after the arrival of European settlers.

✚ 144 D3 ✉ 675 Belleville Street, Victoria
☎ 250/356-7226 🕐 Daily 9–5,
Fri and Sat until 10pm ✋ Expensive
🍴 Café on site

10 Stanley Park

www.vancouver.ca/parks

Few city parks are as wild or beautiful as Vancouver's Stanley Park, a captivating medley of forest, lakes, beaches and pretty formal gardens.

The park crowns the western tip of Vancouver's downtown peninsula, a sublime green counterpoint to the ranks of glass-and-steel skyscrapers close by. One of the city's great glories, it was set aside as early as 1888, when it was saved for posterity in the name of Lord Stanley, Canada's governor general from 1888 to 1893. Thus was preserved North America's largest urban park (it is 20 percent larger than New York's Central Park), an area that in many places looks much as Vancouver must have looked before the arrival of Europeans.

Some is still forest, barely penetrable and dotted with vast, ancient trees; some has been tamed, and turned into lawns and formal gardens; and some has been set aside for attractions such as the Vancouver Aquarium

(► 65), **Children's Farmyard** and **Miniature Railway.** There's even a cricket pitch, a lagoon, a lake, and some fine beaches, one of which (Second Beach) has a popular swimming pool

The best way to see the park is on foot or by bicycle (there are several rental outlets at the corner of Denman and West Georgia streets near the park entrance): there is also a shuttle bus in summer. Whether on foot or bicycle, most people follow all or part of the Seawall, a promenade that runs round the park's waterfront perimeter for around 8km (5 miles). If you want to escape, however, there are plenty of quieter paths in the park's interior.

🚹 142 D4 ⊠ Entrances at West Georgia Street, Robson Street, Stanley Park Drive and elsewhere ☎ Park 604/257-8400 or 604/681-6728 🕒 Always open 🎟 Free 🍴 Sequoia Grill at the Teahouse, Fish House at Stanley Park 🚌 19 to Stanley Park Loop or 240, 241, 246 and other services along West Georgia Street

Children's Farmyard
☎ 604/257-8531 🕒 Call or see website for hours 🎟 Inexpensive

Miniature Railway
☎ 604/257-8531 🕒 Call or see website for times and special services 🎟 Inexpensive

Exploring

Vancouver is a pleasure to explore, with most of its attractions accessible on foot, and virtually all of them framed by a backdrop that combines the sparkling waters of the Pacific and the soaring, forest-covered slopes of the Coast Mountains. Across the island-dotted Strait of Georgia, on Vancouver Island, is Victoria, the provincial capital of British Columbia, a much smaller and more traditional city than cosmopolitan Vancouver. In British Columbia, the vast and spectacularly beautiful Canadian province that stretches from the sea to the Canadian Rockies, the long distances and large areas of wilderness make exploring more difficult. But the roads are excellent, and in a car – or by Greyhound bus – it's possible to get a taste of the region, even on a short visit. If your time is very limited, however, devote most of your trip to the Canadian Rockies, whose four major national parks are surprisingly easy to explore.

Vancouver

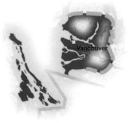

Vancouver is an immediately likeable city: accessible, easy to grasp, and easy to explore. It has plenty of sights, as well as great shopping, nightlife and dining opportunities, but much of its appeal comes from its setting and surroundings. Be sure simply to walk in its parks and gardens, or along its beaches and waterfront promenades, to appreciate its amazing natural beauty.

Most of what you want to see is in the downtown core, a peninsula bordered by the waters of the Burrard Inlet to the north and False Creek to the south, and capped in the west by the wonderful expanse of Stanley Park. To the east of downtown are Gastown, the renovated heart of the 19th-century city, and Chinatown, which boasts one of North America's largest Chinese communities. Across the Burrard Inlet, in the shadow of the mountains, is the North Shore, or North Vancouver, reached by SeaBus ferry or by road across the Lions Gate Bridge. South of False Creek, the mostly residential suburbs of South Vancouver stretch away to the Fraser River and beyond.

The best place to start a tour is Canada Place, right on the water and by the main visitor center. From here it is easy to walk through much of downtown, or head east to Gastown or west to Stanley Park. Definitely devote at least a day to North Vancouver, and Grouse Mountain in particular, and to Yaletown and Granville Island – and the nearby museums of Vanier Park – on the southern edge of downtown. Farther afield, also be sure to see the Museum of Anthropology, a bus or taxi ride away on the city's university campus.

www.tourismvancouver.com

✠ 134 D2 🛈 TouristInfo Centre, 200 Burrard Street ☎ 604/683-2000

CANADA PLACE

Best places to see, ➤ 24–25.

CAPILANO RIVER

The Capilano is one of several short, tumultuous rivers that drain the mountains above North Vancouver, running just 32km (20 miles) before emptying into the Burrard Inlet west of the Lions Gate Bridge. The Capilano River Regional Park protects much of the river's last 10km (6 miles), embracing a medley of canyons, forest and pretty riverside trails. All of it is easily accessible, and is best combined with a visit to the nearby Grouse Mountain (➤ 28–29).

The northernmost attraction, about 1km (0.6 miles) from Grouse Mountain, is the Cleveland Dam, built in 1954, which provides around 40 percent of Vancouver's drinking water. Walk across for lovely views of Capilano Lake below, plus a choice of easy riverside and other trails on the far bank. The best of these is the Giant Fir Trail, but you could equally walk downstream toward the river's second main sight, the **Capilano Salmon Hatchery**. This was built in 1971 to help the river's salmon and replenish stocks damaged by the dam, which destroyed 95 percent of the salmon spawning territory. It is a fascinating place, with the chance to watch leaping salmon and learn about their remarkable life cycle. Pretty trails run up and downstream from the main hatchery complex.

Most people visiting the Capilano River aim for the 137m (450ft) **Capilano Suspension Bridge** – the world's longest pedestrian suspension bridge. While it offers dizzying views of the Capilano Gorge way below, it's as well to note that the attraction is expensive and busy, receiving almost a million visitors a year. The site also offers numerous tours, places to eat and minor attractions, notably the Treetops adventure, a series of bridges and walkways above the forest floor.

www.gvrd.bc.ca

www.capbridge.com

✚ 143 B5 🚌 SeaBus then bus 236 from Lonsdale Quay

Capilano Salmon Hatchery

✉ 4500 Capilano Park Road ☎ 604/666-1790 🕐 Jun–Aug daily 8–8; May, Sep daily 8–7; Apr, Oct daily 9–4:45; Nov–Mar daily 8–4 ✋ Free

Capilano Suspension Bridge

✉ 3735 Capilano Road ☎ 604/985-7474 🕐 Apr daily 9–6:30; May, Jun, Sep daily 8:30–8; Jul–Aug daily 8:30am–9pm; Oct daily 9–6; Nov–Mar daily 9–5 ✋ Expensive 🍴 Café on site

CHINATOWN

With more than 100,000 inhabitants, Vancouver's Chinatown district, to the east of Gastown and downtown, is one of the world's largest, comparable to the similar communities in New York and San Francisco. Most of the area's original inhabitants came to Canada during British Columbia's 1858 gold rush, or to seek work shortly afterward on the transcontinental Canadian Pacific Railway. Many of the immigrants were marginalized and discriminated against, but in Chinatown's clan associations and tight-knit community they found a welcoming refuge.

More than 150 years later, Chinatown is still almost entirely Chinese, full of bakeries, herbal medicine outlets and tiny stores selling exotic fruits and vegetables. There's also a vibrant night market in summer. Most signs are in Chinese, streets buzz with activity and Chinese conversation, and most of the buildings are laden with Chinese architectural details. It's a great area to wander, but make a point of visiting the 1913 Sam Kee Building (corner of Carrall and Pender streets): at just 1.8m (5ft 10in) across, it's claimed to be the world's narrowest building.

Also be sure to visit the **Chinese Cultural Centre,** which offers insights into the area's history, and the quarter's main attraction, the delightful **Dr. Sun Yat-Sen Garden.** It is named for the founder of the Chinese Republic, who made three fundraising visits to Vancouver in 1897, 1910 and 1911. Built with Chinese assistance for Expo '86 (► 24), it was the first classical-style Chinese garden in the West, and is a harmonious blend of plantings and space.

Do note that much of Chinatown is rather down-at-heel, and that you should avoid walking the backstreets at night.

www.vancouverchinesegarden.com

www.cccvan.com

✚ 143 E6 🚇 Stadium 🚌 10, 16, 20 ❓ Free 45-min guided tours of the garden every half-hour (daily 4–8pm)

Chinese Cultural Centre

✉ 555 Columbia Street ☎ 604/658-8880 or 604/658-8850 🕓 Tue–Sun 11–5 👋 Inexpensive 🍴 Café on site ❓ Cultural Centre tours and workshops are available (inexpensive)

Dr. Sun Yat-Sen Garden

✉ 578 Carrall Street at Pender Street ☎ 604/662-3207 🕓 Garden mid-Jun to Aug daily 9:30–7; May to mid-Jun, Sep daily 10–6; Oct–Apr daily 10–4:30 👋 Moderate 🍴 Café on site

CHRIST CHURCH CATHEDRAL

Vancouver's first church service took place – without a church – on Granville Street in 1888, a month before a committee convened to raise funds for the present Christ Church Cathedral, completed in 1895. Offering a striking architectural contrast to the surrounding skyscrapers, the neo-Gothic building is clad in sandstone, but is built on a framework of massive timbers culled from the now-vanished forests of present-day South Vancouver. The lovely interior provides a calm refuge from the bustle of the downtown streets.

www.cathedral.vancouver.bc.ca

✚ 142 C2 ✉ 690 Burrard Street and West Georgia Street ☎ 604/682-3848 🕔 Visiting hours Mon–Fri 9:30–4, Sat 9:30–4:30, Sun 1–5; longer hours for services 🖐 Free 🚇 Burrard 🚌 98

COAL HARBOUR SEAWALK

The building of Canada Place in 1986 was the start of an extensive period of redevelopment of the downtown waterfront, a process that continues to this day. Some of the most striking changes have occurred around Coal Harbour, toward Stanley Park, an area now filled with open public spaces and ranks of attractive residential high-rise buildings. Now that most projects are nearing completion, it has been possible to create the Coal Harbour Seawalk, an unbroken waterfront promenade that provides a delightful pedestrian approach to Stanley Park or the West End from close to Canada Place and the downtown core.

✚ 142 C2 ✉ Coal Harbour Seawalk

CYPRESS PROVINCIAL PARK

Cypress Provincial park is the most westerly of parks in North Vancouver, approached via the Cypress Parkway (which offers fine views), 15km (9.3 miles) north off exit 8 on Hwy 1-99 at Cypress Bowl Road. Although you'll need a car (or taxi) to get here, the majority of visitors come to walk the park's many trails, most of which start from the car park at the top of the Parkway. These include the easy Yew Lake (2km/1.2 miles round-trip; 45 mins) and Black Mountain Loop (2.5km/1.5 miles, 45 mins, 100m/328ft elevation gain). All the trails are well-marked and provide quick and easy access to beautiful forest, lakes and upland meadows. In winter, the park is a popular winter sports destination.

www.cypressmountain.ca

✠ 134 D2 ⊠ Cypress Bowl Road ☎ Park 604/924-2200, winter sports 604/926-5612 🕐 Daily 24 hours 💵 Free

ENGLISH BAY

English Bay is one of the reasons the West End (➤ 71) is one of Vancouver's most popular residential districts. Fringed by beaches and parks, it is perfect for strolling, sunbathing, people-watching or admiring the sunset. Better still, it's easily seen after visiting Stanley Park, or as the culmination of a stroll along the bustling Denman Street with its many cafés, restaurants and appealing shops. It's especially attractive in the early evening, when the bar of the Sylvia Hotel, among others, is a popular rendezvous. Don't miss the bay's 6m-high (20ft) Inukshuk sculpture, an Inuit sign of welcome and the symbol of the 2010 Vancouver Winter Olympics.

✠ 142 E4 🚍 5, 6

GASTOWN

Gastown is the original heart of modern Vancouver, and takes its name from "Gassy" Jack Deighton, a talkative and hard-living publican who, in the 1860s, opened a bar close to the present-day site of Maple Tree Square. In those days, the area was little more than a clearing in the forest, and the bar served the loggers and workers at local saw mills, where alcohol was prohibited. In time, a shanty town – Gassy's Town – grew up around the bar, renamed Granville in 1869. In 1886 the little town was renamed Vancouver, only for its mostly wooden buildings to burn to the ground in the same year.

Rebuilding commenced immediately, but this time in stone, producing the largely late-Victorian district you see today. Much of the area has been renovated, Gastown having fallen into disrepair during the 20th century as the focus of the city moved west to the current downtown core. Today it is a fun and charming area

to wander, many of the bland souvenir shops that opened in the immediate aftermath of renovation having now been replaced by more interesting fashion boutiques, design stores and galleries of Inuit and other art.

Water Street is the main thoroughfare, home to a famous little steam-powered clock, The Landing (a small, upscale mall), and Maple Tree Square, where you'll find several small cafés and a statue of Gassy Jack sitting on a whiskey barrel. A little to the east is the **Vancouver Police Centennial Museum,** housed in the city's old Coroner's Court Building. A fun – and slightly bizarre – museum, it offers an often eye-opening insight into crime and policing in the city, as well the original morgue and autopsy room, complete with preserved body parts.

✚ 142 C3 🚇 Waterfront 🚌 4, 6, 7, 8

Vancouver Police Centennial Museum

✉ 240 East Cordova Street ☎ 604/665-3346 🕒 Mon–Sat 9–5
✋ Inexpensive

GRANVILLE ISLAND
Best places to see, ➤ 26–27.

GROUSE MOUNTAIN
Best places to see, ➤ 28–29.

GULF ISLANDS
Not everyone will have time to visit the Gulf Islands, the archipelago in the waters of the Strait of Georgia between Vancouver and Vancouver Island. But if you're lucky enough to be spending a couple of weeks in the region, try to find time to see at least one of the islands, possibly Salt Spring or Galiano, the most easily accessible from Vancouver, or quieter Pender and Mayne.

Even if you don't have time to visit, you'll see many of the islands, large and small, if you're traveling between Vancouver and Victoria. Seaplanes (➤ 14) offer wonderful aerial views of the islands, as do the ships of BC Ferries as they ply the route from Tsawwassen (the ferry terminal south of Vancouver) to Swartz Bay on Vancouver Island (the terminal for Victoria).

All the islands share similar characteristics, being fringed with small bays and beaches, and with unspoiled interior countryside of hills, forest, smallholdings and peaceful back roads. The idyllic pastoral setting and easy-going pace of life have attracted many artists and writers, as well as those seeking an alternative to city living. As a result, the villages and countryside are scattered with galleries, farm shops, organic stores and craft and artisans' workshops.

As a visitor, it's easy to slip into the island way of life, enjoying coffee and homemade cakes at a little café, idling on the beach,

taking an easy hike, browsing the galleries or renting a bike to explore the many quiet country lanes. Fishing, sailing and other water sports are also widely available. Accommodations are mainly B&Bs, or the odd small inn or hotel, and can be found using the official island and other websites (➤ below). But book early as the islands are very popular in summer.

www.saltspringtourism.com

www.galianoisland.com

www.mayneislandchamber.ca

www.penderislandchamber.com

www.bcferries.com

🕂 134 E2 🛳 BC Ferries services to all islands from Tsawwassen

❓ Accommodations information www.hellobc.com or www.gulfislandsreservations.com

ℹ Saltspring Visitor Centre, 121 Lower Ganges Road ☎ 250/537-5252 or 250/537-4223

H.R. MACMILLAN SPACE CENTRE

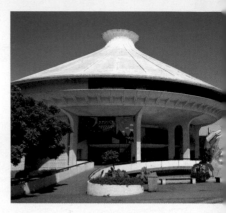

This high-tech museum and planetarium delve into all aspects of space and space travel, and provide a failsafe attraction for most children. They're also easily seen in conjunction with the Vancouver Museum next door (► 68–69) and the Vancouver Maritime Museum (► 68), a short walk away across Vanier Park. Arrive early, however, as the many innovative, hands-on displays are popular, and the center can become crowded.

Among the attractions are displays that allow you to plan a trip to Mars, grapple with aliens, guide a lunar probe, design a rocket and (in the Virtual Voyages Simulator) gain some idea of what it actually feels like to be aboard a spaceship. The Ground Station Canada theater also presents interesting 20-minute films on space-related themes.

The planetarium offers star shows (usually in the afternoons), but the more dynamic evening laser shows, accompanied by music, are very popular, so arrive promptly or be sure to book tickets. A short way from the center is the Gordon Southam Observatory, which – weather allowing – the public can use for star-gazing at weekends. Entry is free, but check current opening times with the Space Centre.

www.hrmacmillanspacecentre.com

✚ 142 D1 ✉ 1100 Chestnut Street at Whyte Avenue ☎ 604/738-7827 🕐 Daily 10–5 (closed Mon Sep–Jun) 💵 Expensive. Laser shows, moderate 🍴 Café 🚌 2, 22 ⛴ Aquabus and False Creek services to Vanier Park ❓ A combined $30 Explorepass (www.vanierpark.com/explorepass.htm) offers entry to the Space Centre, Vancouver Museum and Vancouver Maritime Museum; buy it from the main visitor center (► 16) and participating sights

KITSILANO

Kitsilano (or Kits) is a leafy residential district that stretches west of Vanier Park on the southern shore of English Bay. Now one of the most desirable places to live in Vancouver, it sprang to fame in the heady days of the 1960s, when it was at the heart of the city's alternative hippy culture. Something of the easygoing air of those days survives – one of the reasons for the area's popularity – especially in the many laid-back cafés, restaurants, galleries and specialist stores. For a taste of the district and its inhabitants, spend an hour or two on Kitsilano Beach, a fine stretch of sand, park and waterfront.

✚ 142 E4 🚌 2, 7, 22, 32, 44

LIGHTHOUSE PARK

Lighthouse Park is for those who have a little longer to spend in the city, as it is the most westerly of the parks dotted across North and West Vancouver. This said, it is easily reached by bus – it is 10km (6 miles) from the Lions Gate Bridge – and offers a taste of the wild seascapes of Canada's west coast. Vast, smooth granite boulders scatter the beach, backed by low bluffs and stands of Douglas fir and other virgin forest. Some 13km (8 miles) of trails wend through the park, including a 5km (3-mile) round-trip to the 1912 Atkinson Lighthouse that gives the park its name.

✚ 142 B1 ✉ Beacon Lane and Marine Drive ☎ 604/925-7200
🕐 Dawn–dusk ♿ Free 🚌 250 from Lonsdale Quay

LONSDALE QUAY

Among other things, Lonsdale Quay is the terminus in North Vancouver for the SeaBus ferries that cross the Burrard Inlet from Waterfront Station on the downtown peninsula. Even if you go no farther than the terminus building, the trip here is worthwhile for the magnificent views of the port and city skyline from the ferry. However, it's well worth budgeting an hour or two for the Lonsdale Quay market, just moments from the SeaBus terminal. While not as alluring as the Granville Island market – few markets are – it is still a great place to browse, with food on the lower of its two levels, and small, specialist stores on the upper. The best thing to do is to choose one of the many cafés or food stands, or to buy provisions from the market for a picnic, and then settle down on the wooden waterfront terraces to enjoy the spectacular panorama of the downtown skyline across the Burrard Inlet. You'll probably also pass through the quay if you are visiting other sights in North Vancouver, for the complex contains the bus terminal for departures to Grouse Mountain and other destinations.

www.lonsdalequay.com

➕ 143 C6 ✉ Lonsdale Quay Market, 123 Carrie Cates Court
☎ 604/985-6261 🕓 Market Mon–Sat 9:30–6:30 (later opening Fri); dining options remain open later 💷 Free 🚢 SeaBus from Waterfront Station

LYNN CANYON PARK

After Grouse Mountain (➤ 28–29) and parts of the Capilano River (➤ 46–47), Lynn Canyon is the place in North Vancouver to visit if you want some gentle hikes and an easily accessible glimpse of the city's wild outdoors. Buses from Lonsdale Quay (▶ opposite) will drop you five or ten minutes' walk from the park entrance, depending on the service (or you can take a taxi). Beyond here, on the left, is the Ecology Centre, which offers videos, natural history displays and hiking and other information.

One of the park's main attractions is a suspension bridge

over a forest canyon. It is not quite as spectacular as its more famous counterpart on the Capilano River, but it is free and far less busy. It's easily reached on one of the park's several trails, the most popular of which are the 15-minute Thirty-Foot Pool and 40-minute Twin Falls trails. Most of the forest here is so-called "second-growth," meaning that it is forest that has regenerated after the original "first-growth" trees have been felled.

www.dnv.org/ecology

🎫 143 B8 ✉ 3663 Park Road, off Peters Road
☎ 604/990-3755 🕐 Park daily 7am–dusk. Ecology Centre Jun–Sep daily 10–5; Oct–May daily 12–5
✋ Park free. Ecology Centre, donation 🍴 Lonsdale Quay 🚌 SeaBus to Lonsdale Quay then bus 228 or 229 to Peters Road (20 mins) ❓ Free guided walks from Ecology Centre Jul–Aug

MARINE BUILDING

Walk a minute or so up Burrard Street from the modern wonders of Canada Place and you come to an older, but equally beguiling architectural fragment. The 25-floor Marine Building dates from 1930, and is one of North America's finest period skyscrapers, thanks largely to its wonderful art deco doorway and facade. The English poet Sir John Betjeman described it as the "best art deco office building in the world."

Its original owners were shipowners and financiers, and the building was intended as a monument in stone to Vancouver's maritime tradition and the importance to the city of its port and seafarers. Thus the beautifully restored facade is studded with numerous bas-reliefs in brass, stone and terra-cotta, including sea creatures, famous ships from history, trains, aircraft, Zeppelins and other sea- and transportation-linked motifs. The equally striking doorway is often used as a backdrop in many of the films and TV shows shot in the city. The lobby also boasts lovely art deco styling, especially the outstanding wood-and-brass elevator doors and the inlaid zodiac floor.

✚ 142 C3 ✉ 355 Burrard Street and West Hastings Street ⊙ Mon–Fri 8–6 ✋ Free 🚇 Burrard 🚌 98

MOUNT SEYMOUR PROVINCIAL PARK

You'll need a car or taxi to reach this park, the largest, wildest and most easterly of the protected areas in North Vancouver. You'll also need to devote a day to the park to make the most of its many excellent hiking and mountain-biking trails. If you're going to walk or bike here, be sure to come properly equipped, as the weather can change for the worse at any time of the year.

Mount Seymour Road provides a scenic approach to the park, and runs for 13km (8 miles) to a parking area that marks the start of several key trails. Along the road are viewpoints (Deep Cove Lookout is the most spectacular), picnic areas and several trailheads for short walks. The best of the hikes at the parking area are the Goldie Lake and Flower Lake loops, each about a 45-minute round-trip. The park's most popular hike is the more demanding Mount Seymour Trail (4km/2.5-mile round-trip, 450m/1,476ft elevation gain; allow two hours), which climbs to the summit of Mount Seymour (1,455m/4,774ft) itself.

www.env.gov.bc.ca/bcparks

✚ 134 D3 ✉ 1700 Mount Seymour Road ☎ 604/986-2261 ⏰ Daily 24 hours ✋ Free 🚌 SeaBus to Lonsdale Quay, then bus 239 to Phibbs Exchange and 215 to Mount Seymour-Indian River ❓ Park maps can be downloaded from the website

MUSEUM OF ANTHROPOLOGY
Best places to see, ➤ 36–37.

NITOBE MEMORIAL GARDEN AND UBC BOTANICAL GARDEN

These two gardens are a 5-minute and 15-minute walk respectively from the Museum of Anthropology (➤ 36–37) on the campus of the University of British Columbia. The Nitobe Memorial Garden is a small Japanese garden named after Dr. Inanzo Nitobe (1862–1933), an academic and supporter of improved pan-Pacific relations. Now more than 40 years old, and considered one of the most perfect gardens of its type outside Japan, it is a beautiful and peaceful spot, its flowers, trees, rocks and other ornamental features carefully placed according to the principles of yin and yang. Take time to wander the gently curving paths, the Tea Garden (where you can take part in a tea ceremony in summer) and the Stroll Garden, designed to represent the journey through life from youth to old age.

Almost opposite the Nitobe Memorial Garden is the larger UBC Botanical Garden, created in 1916, making it Canada's oldest botanical garden. It has more than 10,000 plants, trees and shrubs, and is divided into eight theme sections: Alpine, Arbour, Asian, British Columbia Native, Contemporary, Food, Perennial Border and Physic. It also has Canada's largest collection of rhododendrons and the outstanding Botanical Garden Shop, full of books, shrubs, plants and gardening implements.

www.nitobe.org

🕂 142 E1 ✉ 1895 Lower Mall, near Gate 4, Memorial Road
☎ 604/822-6038 ⏰ Nitobe Memorial Garden: mid-Mar to Oct daily 9–5;
Nov to mid-Mar Mon–Fri 10–2:30. UBC Botanical Garden: mid-Mar to mid-Oct
daily 10–6; mid-Oct to mid-Mar daily 10–4 💰 Both gardens, inexpensive;
both by donation mid-Oct to mid-Mar 🚌 4, 17, 44 then 10-min walk ❓ Joint
ticket moderate

QUEEN ELIZABETH PARK

Vancouver's third-largest park had inauspicious origins, beginning life as quarries for the Canadian Pacific Railway (CPR) in the 19th century. After remaining derelict for years, the Quarry Gardens were landscaped in 1930, providing the impetus for the creation of a larger surrounding park, completed in 1939. The area centers on the so-called Little Mountain, which at 153m (502ft) is the highest point in South Vancouver, providing panoramic views over the city toward the mountains of North Vancouver. A winding road leads to the summit, passing through an arboretum that contains most of the trees and shrubs native to British Columbia. Another highlight is the Bloedel Conservatory, an indoor space that replicates the climate and some of the flora and fauna of desert, subtropical and rain forest habitats. The conservatory offers a 360-degree vista, as well as some 500 varieties of plants and 50 species of birds.

✚ 143 F5 ✉ West 33rd Avenue at Cambie Street ☎ 604/257-8584
🕐 Daily 24 hours 🚇 King Edward Canada Line 🚌 15

SCIENCE WORLD

This is an essential stop for anyone traveling with children, thanks to its innovative interactive and other displays, all of them designed to make science fun and accessible. The vast silver geodesic dome in which it is housed is one of the most distinctive features of the city's skyline, and is one of the key survivors – with Canada Place – of the many striking structures built for Expo '86 (➤ 24). Inside the rambling, open-plan building are five major galleries spread over two levels, plus a large OMNIMAX movie theater on the third level. There's also a special section for children under six, along with regular science shows and demonstrations, usually child-pleasing events with lots of bangs and explosions.

Be warned that the complex is very popular, especially on rainy days and during school terms. It is also a little to the east of the downtown core, so you'll need to take a taxi or SkyTrain to get here, though the latter should be a small adventure in itself for young children.

www.scienceworld.bc.ca

✚ 142 D3 ✉ 1455

Québec Street at Terminal Avenue ☎ 604/443-7440. Recorded information 604/443-7443 🕙 Mon–Fri 10–5, Sat–Sun 10–6 💰 Expensive. OMNIMAX, moderate. Combined Science World-Omnimax tickets available 🍽 White Spot restaurant ($) on site 🚇 Main Street-Science World 🚌 3

STANLEY PARK

Best places to see, ➤ 40–41.

VANCOUVER AQUARIUM

With more than a million visitors a year, the Vancouver Aquarium is the most popular visitor attraction in Canada west of Toronto's CN Tower. At the heart of Stanley Park, it features around 60,000 living exhibits and some 6,000 marine species. Criticism from animal rights campaigners has helped encourage a move toward more scientific research, but the highlights here are still those of aquariums the world over – performing dolphin shows. Also hugely popular are the beluga whales, whose cramped pool has also aroused controversy. Less contentious are some of the underground galleries, where tanks contain all manner of exotic and extraordinary smaller sea creatures. Various areas are also given over to different marine habitats, including wetlands, Arctic Canada and the Amazon rain forest. The aquarium is relatively small, and it can become very crowded, especially around the dolphin pool and in the underground galleries.

www.vanaqua.org

✚ 143 D5 ✉ 845 Avison Way, Stanley Park ☎ 604/659-3474 🕐 Daily 9:30–7 (closes 5pm Oct–Apr) 💷 Expensive 🍴 On-site café 🚌 19, then 10-min walk

VANCOUVER ART GALLERY

Vancouver's main public art gallery comes as something of a surprise, for, unlike most mainstream city galleries, it largely ignores traditional paintings in favor of often challenging temporary exhibitions and a permanent collection largely devoted to contemporary art – photography in particular. As admission is expensive, it pays to be sure of the current exhibitions ahead of visiting. Little in the traditional exterior suggests the striking modern art inside, the gallery having originally been the city's main courthouse, completed in 1911 and converted by Vancouver-born Arthur Erickson, one of Canada's leading architects, in 1983.

For casual visitors, the gallery's main attractions are likely to be the paintings of Emily Carr (1871–1945), born in Victoria and one of Canada's best-known and best-loved painters. Landscape and First Nations culture heavily influenced her work, which is distinguished by vivid colors and powerful, sometimes almost surreal images.

Plans are under way for a new venue for the gallery in a waterside setting on False Creek's Plaza of Nations.

www.vanartgallery.bc.ca

🞧 142 C2 ✉ 750 Hornby Street at Robson Street ☎ 604/662-4700, recorded information 604/662-4719 🕐 Mon, Wed, Fri–Sun, public holidays 10–5:30, Tue, Thu 10–9 ✋ Expensive, by donation Tue 5–9 🍴 Gallery Café ($) 🚇 Granville 🚌 5, 50 to Robson Street or 2, 22, 32, 44 to Burrard Street ❓ Admission free (or by donation) Tue 5–9pm

VANCOUVER LOOKOUT

Vancouver is a city of mountains, ocean and tall buildings, and therefore also a city blessed with an unusually large number of wonderful views and viewpoints. One of the best urban eyries is the Vancouver Lookout, at the top of the Harbour Centre Tower, located between Canada Place and the fringes of Gastown. Neil Armstrong, the first man on the moon, opened the tower in 1977, when – at 167m (548ft) – it was the city's highest building. All-glass elevators, known as the SkyLift, run up the outside of the tower, climbing the building in under a minute and offering a dizzying initial panorama over the city. The views are even better from the viewing platform, which also contains a restaurant (the ride up is free if you have dining reservations here) and lots of information boards and fascinating period photographs that show how the view and its buildings have changed over the decades. The admission ticket is valid all day (keep your receipt), so consider coming back to watch the sun go down and to admire the city at night.

www.vancouverlookout.com

➕ 142 C3 ✉ 555 West Hastings Street at Seymour Street ☎ 604/689-0421, restaurant 604/669-2220 🕐 May to mid-Oct daily 8:30am–10:30pm; mid-Oct to Apr daily 9–9 💷 Moderate 🍴 Top of Vancouver Revolving Restaurant ($$) on site 🚇 Waterfront 🚌 4, 6, 7, 8, 50 ❓ Tickets are valid for return visits all day

VANCOUVER MARITIME MUSEUM

This traditional-style and modest-size museum explores Vancouver's long and vital maritime tradition through photographs, charts, maps, model ships and a wide variety of other marine ephemera. Located in Vanier Park, it is easily visited with the Vancouver Museum (► below) and H.R. MacMillan Space Centre (► 56).

The best approach is aboard one of the small ferries that run from Granville Island and other points on False Creek. They dock in Vanier Park at Heritage Harbour, so called because it contains a range of restored historic boats. From here it's a short walk to the museum, where the highlight is the *St. Roch*, a Royal Canadian Mounted Police schooner that was the first vessel to navigate the Northwest Passage (the ice-filled route across the roof of North America) in a single season. Youngsters will enjoy the Pirates' Cove and Children's Maritime Discovery Centre, full of interactive displays, telescopes trained on the harbor and fun costumes for dressing up.

www.vancouvermaritimemuseum.com

➕ 142 D1 ✉ 1905 Ogden Avenue at Chestnut Street ☎ 604/257-8300 🕒 May–Aug daily 10–5; Sep–Apr Tue–Sat 10–5, Sun noon–5 ✋ Moderate 🍴 Café in Vancouver Museum 🚌 2, 22 ⛴ Aquabus and False Creek services from Granville Island ❓ Combined ticket ($30) with H.R. MacMillan Space Centre (► 56) and Vancouver Museum

VANCOUVER MUSEUM

If you're short of time in Vancouver, but are planning to visit Victoria, then you might want to pass on the Vancouver Museum in favor of the latter city's Royal BC Museum (► 38–39), which covers much the same ground – the history of Vancouver, Victoria and British Columbia – with more panache. If not, then this museum does a reasonable job of tracing Vancouver's aboriginal roots and more recent past, combining a chronological approach with numerous themed displays and lots of period artifacts. Particularly good is the section devoted to immigration, including part of a reconstructed ship that reveals the conditions most of the poorest immigrants would have faced crossing the oceans to their new lives.

www.vanmuseum.bc.ca

➕ 142 D1 ✉ 1100 Chestnut Street at Whyte Avenue ☎ 604/736-4431 🕐 Jul–Sep Mon–Wed, Fri–Sun 10–5, Thu 5–9pm. Closed Mon Oct–Jun 🍴 Café on site 🚌 2, 22 🚢 Aquabus and False Creek Ferries services to Vanier Park 👋 Expensive ❓ Combined Explorepass ($30) includes Vancouver Maritime Museum and H.R. MacMillan Space Centre

VANCOUVER PUBLIC LIBRARY

Nowhere is the booming confidence of modern Vancouver, or the degree to which its old downtown core is expanding, better illustrated than in its majestic public library. Opened in 1995 at a cost of $100 million (making it the most expensive public building ever constructed in the city), it is the centerpiece of a residential redevelopment project that is reaching south from downtown toward Yaletown (➤ 72) and False Creek. It resembles a latter-day Roman Colosseum, though architect Moshe Safdi apparently denies this was intentional, and is surrounded by an attractive plaza that buzzes with people and activity. Go inside, if you have time, to admire the interior and the views from the upper floors.

www.vpl.ca

➕ 142 D3 ✉ 350 West Georgia Street at Robson and Homer streets ☎ 604/331-3601 🕐 Mon–Thu 10–9, Fri–Sat 10–6, Sun 1–6 👋 Free

VANDUSEN BOTANICAL GARDEN

Like the nearby Queen Elizabeth Park (➤ 63), the VanDusen
Botanical Garden may be too far south of the city center for
most casual visitors, but is well worth the journey if you have
even the slightest horticultural interest. Many critics rate it as
among the ten best botanical gardens in North America. The site
contains thousands of plants, trees and shrubs from around the
world, including a number of theme areas such as Rose, Lake
and Rhododendron gardens. The displays are designed so that
there is something to see in all months of the year. The popular
Elizabethan Hedge Maze is made up of 1,000 pyramid cedars,
each no more than 1.5m (4ft 9in) high so adults can keep track of
their children from a grassy knoll as they navigate the labyrinth.
www.vandusengarden.org

✚ 143 F5 ✉ 5251 Oak Street at West 33rd Avenue and West 37th Avenue
☎ 604/878-9274 🕓 Mar, Oct daily 10–5; Apr daily 10–6; Jun–Aug daily
10–9; Sep daily 10–7; Nov–Feb daily 10–4 ✋ Moderate (inexpensive
Oct–Mar) 🍴 Café on site 🚇 King Edward Canada Line 🚌 17 to Oak Street

WATERFRONT STATION

Today, Waterfront Station is a major terminus for the SkyTrain
light transit and for the SeaBus ferry services to Lonsdale Quay
in North Vancouver. The imposing building it occupies, however,
was formerly the western terminus of a far grander transportation
link, the transcontinental Canadian Pacific Railway (the new bus
and rail terminus is now housed in a bland part of the city to the
southeast). Behind the imposing neoclassical facade (1915) is a
concourse filled with shops, though it still contains original murals
depicting various landscapes that passengers would have seen as
they crossed Canada on the railway. The *Angel of Victory* (1922)
statue in front of the station is dedicated to CPR staff who lost
their lives in World War I.

✚ 142 C3 ✉ 601 West Cordova Street at Granville Street

WEST END

The West End is the name given to the leafy residential district between Stanley Park and the main downtown core. Centered on Robson and Burrard streets, it has always been a desirable area in which to live, but received a new lease of life in the 1950s when the city council promoted new, low-rise buildings in the area to encourage a viable inner-city district. Several older historic fragments survive, notably Barclay Square and **Roedde House,** along with dazzling now developments, notably to the north along the Coal Harbour waterfront (➤ 50). Denman Street is the area's main nonresidential axis, full of cafés and shops, and leads to the beach and pretty waterfront park bordering English Bay (➤ 51).

🚇 142 C2 🚌 5 to Robson Street and Denman Street or 6 along Davie Street

Roedde House

www.roeddehouse.org

✉ 1415 Barclay Square ☎ 604/684-7040 🕐 Tue–Sat 1–5, Sun 2–4
✋ Inexpensive 🍴 Cafés on Denman and Davie streets

YALETOWN

Previously a rundown warehouse district, today Yaletown is a completely revitalized area full of trendy loft apartments, great restaurants, boutique hotels and interesting shops and galleries. It takes its name from the laborers who moved here from the town of Yale, 180km (112 miles) east of Vancouver, as work on the transcontinental railway ended in the 1880s. It was a lawless enclave, too rough even for the Mounties to control: it apparently contained more saloons per acre than anywhere else on earth.

Today, the area is easily explored, and centers on a small grid of streets around Homer, Mainland and Hamilton, with Drake to the south and Smithe to the north (the streets to the west and north are relatively uninteresting). Gentrification has not taken away the area's slightly gritty charm, most obvious in the raised walkways once used to facilitate loading from the warehouses beyond.

It's a fun area to wander at random, either by day or night (there are lots of bars for an evening drink or meal) but do drop by **The Roundhouse,** once used to turn locomotives and now home to a cultural center and Engine 374, the steam locomotive that pulled the first passenger train into Vancouver in 1887.

You could walk to Yaletown from downtown via Vancouver Public Library (➤ 69), but another fun approach is to come here on one of the small ferries from Granville Island (➤ 26–27); alternatively, you might stop off en route from Granville Island to Science World to the east (➤ 64).

➕ 142 D2 🚌 4, 6, 7, 10, 16, 17 🚇 Yaletown-Roundhouse new Canada Line

The Roundhouse

✉ Roundhouse Mews at Davie Street and Pacific Boulevard ☎ 604/713-1800; www.roundhouse.ca ⏰ Hours vary ✋ Free 🍴 Many local cafés

Victoria

**BC's charming provincial
capital is the perfect
antidote to Vancouver,
a small and intimate
city, full of quaint streets,
gardens, appealing shops and
plenty of fascinating sights and
attractions. It also has good restaurants and one
of North America's finest museums, as well as an
attractive waterfront and a delightful old quarter.**

□ Victoria

By seaplane, you could see the city as a day trip from Vancouver,
but there's more than enough here to warrant at least an
overnight stay. The city was originally a Salish First Nations village,
but in 1842 became the site of a fort and trading post for the
Hudson's Bay Company. By 1866, this had become a small town
and the capital of British Columbia, a role it retained even after the
coming of the transcontinental railway transformed the fortunes
of Vancouver. Today, the city still has the genteel charm of a
well-kept English country town – one of its attractions, especially
for US visitors – and is a busy, prosperous but still unspoiled place
usually beloved by locals and visitors alike.

✚ 134 F2 🛈 812 Wharf Street ☎ 250/953-2033

ART GALLERY OF GREATER VICTORIA

If you've seen and liked the paintings of Emily Carr in the Vancouver Art Gallery (➤ 66), then it's well worth making the short journey to this gallery just east of the city center. One of Canada's best-known artists, Carr was born in Victoria in 1871, and had an adventurous and bohemian life, studying in Paris and traveling extensively, particularly in the wilds of British Columbia, whose landscapes and First Nations peoples greatly influenced her bold and powerful paintings.

As well as a handful of works by Carr, this modest gallery also has an outstanding collection of Japanese art, along with one of the few complete Shinto shrines outside Japan. There are also numerous temporary exhibitions, and the gallery's home, the 1890 Spencer mansion, is one of the city's more attractive period houses. Note that the gallery is easily seen in conjunction with Craigdarroch Castle (➤ 78), located 200m (220yds) to the east.

www.aggv.bc.ca

🕂 144 C4 (off map) 🖂 1040 Moss Street, off Fort Street ☎ 250/384-4101 🕔 Mon–Sat 10–5 (Thu until 9pm), Sun 1–5. Closed Mon Oct–Apr 🍴 Café ✋ Moderate 🚌 10, 11, 14

BEACON HILL PARK

Victoria is known as the "City of Gardens," and some of the best are found here, in the city's largest park, a few minutes' walk south of the Inner Harbour. In the past, the local Salish peoples knew the area as Meeacan, or "The Belly," because the hill was thought to resemble the large stomach of a man lying on his back.

Today, the park is a mixture of manicured lawns and gardens combined with open spaces and stands of trees, some of them majestic "first-growth" timbers usually found only in regions of Vancouver Island's west coast untouched by foresters. Also here are a cricket pitch, one of the world's tallest totem poles, and the "Mile Zero" marker (the western limit) of the Trans-Canada Highway (Hwy 1). Best of all, though, are the many quiet corners and superb views from the park's southern reaches across the Juan de Fuca Strait to the coast and Olympic Mountains of Washington State in the US.

➕ 144 F3

BUTCHART GARDENS

Best places to see, ➤ 22–23.

a walk

through the historic heart of old Victoria

Central Victoria is a compact area of streets, shops and squares. To see some of the city's green spaces, this walk can be extended south to take in Beacon Hill Park (➤ 75).

Start at the visitor center at the corner of Government and Humboldt streets. Turn left and follow Wharf Street north four blocks before turning right and up steps to Bastion Square.

Bastion Square is the site of the original Fort Victoria. Visit the Maritime Museum (➤ 82) and perhaps have a healthy drink in Rebar.

Turn left on Langley Street on the right-hand side of the Maritime Museum, then left on Yates Street. Cross Yates Street and take the first little alley on the right to emerge on Johnson Street.

Behind the north side of Johnson Street is Market Square, with its many interesting specialist shops.

Exit Market Square on its north side, on Pandora Avenue, and take Fan Tan Alley, a narrow street left (north) off Pandora Avenue, part of Victoria's once bustling Chinatown district. At the end of the alley turn right on Fisgard Street, then right down the main Government Street. Walk three blocks and then turn right down tiny Trounce Alley.

Trounce Alley was once full of bars and brothels, but is now a pretty, narrow street of interesting shops.

Wend south on the backstreets rather than Government Street, turning right at the end of Trounce Alley on Broad Street, then almost immediately left on View Street. Turn right on Douglas Street, first right on Fort and then first left on Broad. Turn right on Broughton and left down Gordon to bring you to Humboldt Street and the Fairmont Empress Hotel.

Distance 2km (1.25 miles)
Time 2 hours, depending on stops
Start/end point Victoria visitor center ✚ 144 D3
Lunch Il Terrazzo

CRAIGDARROCH CASTLE

This sombre Gothic pastiche of a Scottish castle was built by Robert Dunsmuir, a Victorian businessman who grew rich on the back of coal mining and other enterprises. The four-floor castle, built close to the highest point in Victoria, was designed to lure his wife from Scotland, and Dunsmuir spent a fortune securing the best craftsmen and the most expensive marble, granite, sandstone and other materials. Unfortunately, he died in 1889, two years into the project, and a year before it was completed. Today you can walk around the 39 rooms, each meticulously decorated and furnished in Victorian period style. Climb the tower's 87 steps for some far-reaching views.

www.craigdarrochcastle.com

➕ 144 C4 (off map) ✉ 1050 Joan Crescent, off Fort Street ☎ 250/592-5323
🕐 Mid-Jun to Aug daily 9–7:30; Sep to mid-Jun daily 10–5 ✋ Moderate
🚌 11, 14

HELMCKEN HOUSE

Helmcken House is Victoria's oldest-surviving home and the oldest house in British Columbia still on its original site. Built in 1852, it belonged to John Helmcken, doctor of what was then called Fort Victoria and a well-connected and respected pillar of the community – he was married to the daughter of Sir James Douglas, then the colony's governor. Dotted around the house, which still looks much as it must have done over 150 years ago, are numerous period artifacts, including some of Helmcken's fearsome-looking medical equipment. Although British Columbia offers many similar "heritage" houses, you still gain a powerful sense of how life was lived here, helped by audio tapes that use actors and actresses to take on the roles of Helmcken and his family. Just behind the house, which lies alongside the Royal British Columbia Museum, is another period building, St. Anne's Pioneer Schoolhouse, built in 1858.

🚹 144 E3 ✉ Belleville Street ☎ 250/361-0021 🕐 May–Oct daily 10–5; Nov–Apr Thu–Mon 11–4 🍴 Café ✋ Inexpensive

INNER HARBOUR

Victoria's strategic position near the southern tip of Vancouver Island is one of the reasons for its development as a city, though even its position would not have been enough for a European settlement to develop here had it not been for the area's fine natural harbor. Today, the inner core of this harbor forms the heart of the city, a small but beautiful curve of waterfront fringed by a pretty promenade.

This is a delightful place to walk and sit at any time, but especially early in the evening, as the sun is going down. The chances are the promenade will be dotted with street performers, including the almost obligatory Scottish piper. Seaplanes land in the harbor, ferries from Seattle and Port Angeles (but not Vancouver) dock here, and the city's main visitor attraction is prominently situated near the harbor's northern edge. The Royal BC Museum (► 38–39) is not far away, set back from the water, as are Victoria's two most distinctive landmarks: the Parliament Buildings (► 84–85) and the Fairmont Empress Hotel, built in 1908.

The Empress is among Canada's most famous hotels, a sister hotel to the Banff Springs, Chateau Lake Louise (► 122–123) and Hotel Vancouver. All were built in the wake of the transcontinental Canadian Pacific Railway (CPR), and designed to entice and accommodate visitors traveling by train. Today the Empress has some delightful lounges, bars and restaurants open to nonresidents, notably the Crystal Lounge, with its Tiffany-glass dome. The hotel's six-course afternoon tea is popular and renowned – despite the very high prices – and should be booked well in advance.

Two blocks back from the harbor, drop into **Emily Carr House,** where the celebrated painter was born in 1871. The building dates from 1864 and has been painstakingly restored and filled with original furniture, including Carr's bed and other period memorabilia.

✚ 144 C2

🛈 812 Wharf Street ☎ 250/953-2033 ⏰ Mid-Jun to Aug daily 8:30–7:30; Sep to mid-Jun daily 9–5

Emily Carr House

www.emilycarr.com

✉ 207 Government Street ☎ 250/383-5843 ⏰ May–Sep Tue–Sat 11–4 ✋ Donation

MARITIME MUSEUM

These days, Victoria's port is far less important than Vancouver's, but in the 19th century, the city and its harbor were a vital point of entry and trade for virtually all of mainland British Columbia. This traditional museum, housed in a delightful heritage building on historic Bastion Square, looks at the city's maritime past using old charts, maps, models and period photographs. It also has a section on the BC Ferries that provide a modern-day lifeline between the province's many islands and up and down its long coast. The building's top floor contains the former vice-admiralty courtroom, which once provided justice for all of British Columbia.

www.mmbc.bc.ca

✚ 144 C3 ✉ 28 Bastion Square ☎ 250/385-4222 ⏱ Mid-Jun to mid-Sep daily 9:30–5; mid-Sep to mid-Jun daily 9:30–4:30 ✋ Moderate

OLD TOWN

Victoria's historic heart is compact and easily explored (▶ 76–77), centering on the grid of streets between Wharf and Douglas, the Inner Harbour to the south and Discovery Street to the north. This site was originally home to the Salish people, who had ten villages in the region, an area Sir George Vancouver described as "the most lovely country that can be imagined." The first white settlers arrived in 1842, among them James Douglas of the Hudson's Bay Company (HBC), who built Fort Camouson (later Fort Victoria) as a garrison and trading point. Boom followed in the 1850s, when the town became a staging post for prospectors heading for the gold fields on the mainland.

Echoes of these earliest days can be found in Bastion Square, site of the original Fort Victoria, but home today, among other things, to the Maritime Museum (➤ opposite). Two blocks to the north is historic Market Square, the old trading heart of the city, now home to 65 or more specialty stores and cafés ranged around an attractive central courtyard.

The north side of the square, on Pandora Street, was once the city's Chinatown (now centered on a small area a little farther north on Fisgard Street). The oldest such community on North America's west coast, it once had a notorious reputation, and was dotted, among other things, with 23 factories processing 40,000kg (88,000lbs) of opium a year for what was then a legitimate trade.

Be sure to wander up and down Government Street, the city's main shopping thoroughfare, but also the smaller streets to either side, many of which have pretty corners that still evoke a little of what the town must have looked and felt like over a century ago.

✚ 144 C3

PARLIAMENT BUILDINGS

There's no mistaking Victoria's Parliament Buildings, the imposing edifice at the southern end of the Inner Harbour that serves as home to British Columbia's provincial legislature. The building was completed in 1897, just in time for Queen Victoria's jubilee (at the then astronomical cost of $923,000). The architect was Francis Rattenbury, who was also responsible for the nearby Empress Hotel and Vancouver's courthouse, now the Vancouver Art Gallery (▶ 66). In later life he would retire to England, only to be murdered in 1935 by his wife and her teenage lover, the family chauffeur.

The well-kept lawns and gardens in front of the building feature a statue of Queen Victoria and a giant sequoia tree, the latter a gift from the state of California. A statue of Sir George Vancouver looks down from the top of the dome, while the main door is guarded by statues of Sir James Douglas, one of the city's early leading lights (▶ 83), and Sir Matthew Baillie Begbie, also known as the "Hanging Judge." The latter acquired a fearsome reputation as the man responsible for law and order during the reckless days of the 1850s' gold rushes. You can take short guided tours of the interior when parliament is not in session, but hours vary: consult the visitor center for the latest open times.

✚ 144 E2 ✉ 501 Belleville Street ☎ 250/387-3046, 250/387-1400 or 1-800-663-7867 ⊘ Guided tours: hours vary ✋ Free

POINT ELLICE HOUSE

Point Ellice House is in less appealing surroundings than Craigdarroch Castle, Victoria's other main period building, but the building itself is a beautifully restored 1861 Victorian-Italianate residence. The interior is among the best preserved of its type in Canada, with a huge collection of Victoriana, largely because the former owners, the O'Reilly family – who lived here from 1867 through to 1974 – barely changed a single detail or item of furnishing in over a century. The best approach is to take one of the small ferries from the Inner Harbour, which drop you at the

dock by the house. When you arrive, take a tour of the interior, walk in the gardens, perhaps try your hand at croquet, and then settle down to afternoon tea on the lawn, weather allowing (booking advisable).

www.pointellicehouse.ca

✚ 144 A1 ✉ 2616 Pleasant Street

☎ 250/380-6506

🕑 Guided tours May–Sep daily 10–4

✋ Inexpensive. Tea and tour from $23

ROYAL BC MUSEUM

Best places to see,
➤ 38–39.

WHALE-WATCHING

Vancouver Island offers some of the best whale-watching opportunities in North America, thanks to its position on the migration route of around 20,000 Pacific gray whales. The creatures pass this way in April and May and from October to December, en route between their breeding, feeding and calving grounds in the waters off Mexico and Alaska. In addition, southern Vancouver Island also boasts minke and humpback whales, plus about 100 resident orca (or "killer") whales. Tofino, on the island's west coast, offers probably the best chance of sightings, but the waters around Victoria are also rich in whales, as well as other marine life such as harbor and Dall's porpoises, harbor or elephant seals and California and Steller sea lions.

The number of companies offering trips has proliferated, and you'll find full details of all the operators at the city's main visitor center (▶ 16). On the whole, it is best to go for companies that

have been established the longest, such as Five Star Charters, Prince of Whales and Seacoast Expeditions. Most offer similar three- or four-hour trips at similar prices (from about $90 per person). The main differences are in the boats offered: Zodiacs are rubber-hulled inflatable craft, and are fast and exhilarating, while covered boats are slower and carry more people, but are more comfortable and have toilet and other facilities. Always take a hat, warm and waterproof clothing and sunscreen, and note that Zodiacs are not suitable for small children, pregnant women and those with back complaints.

www.5starwhales.com

www.princeofwhales.com

www.seacoastexpeditions.com

✉ Five Star Charters, 706 Douglas Street ☎ 250/388-7223 or 1-800/634-9617 ✉ Prince of Whales, 812 Wharf Street ☎ 250/383-4884 or 1-888/383-4884 ✉ Seacoast Expeditions, Coast Victoria Harbourside Hotel, 146 Kingston Street ☎ 250/383-2254 or 1-800/386-1525 ⏰ Most companies offer between three and five 3- or 4-hour trips daily Jun–Sep, one or two daily Oct–May ✋ From $90 for a 3-hour trip

British Columbia

British Columbia is Canada at its best, a vast province with some of North America's greatest and most varied scenery, from the Rockies and Columbia Mountains in the east, through immense forests, pastoral farming country and areas of near desert, to the majestic coastal landscapes in the east.

British Columbia covers a colossal area – larger than several US states or European countries combined – and no short visit can do it justice. In an ideal world, you would take several days to travel across the south of the region, between Vancouver and the Rockies, following a meandering path taking in the Kootenays, a pristine enclave of mountains and timeless lakeside villages, and the Okanagan, a mild-weathered region of dulcet lakes, orchards, vineyards and busy resort towns. If you have more time, venture into the depths of Wells Gray Provincial Park.

Kamloops

FRASER CANYON

Traveling east from Vancouver, you have a choice of three routes at the town of Hope, about 150km (93 miles) east of the city. One is the fast Hwy 5 to Kamloops via Merritt; the second is Hwy 3, shadowing the US border (➤ 94–95); and the third is the Trans-Canada Highway (Hwy 1) along the Fraser River.

The last is a spectacular drive (or rail journey), following the arduous route taken by the explorer Simon Fraser (1776–1862), who gave his name to the river, having traveled its entire 1,300km (807-mile) length and passed, as he later wrote, "where no man should venture."

Hope is a charming riverside town, best known latterly as one of the settings for *First Blood*, the first Rambo movie, starring Sylvester Stallone. Consult the visitor center for information on fishing, canoeing and gold panning locally, or pick up details of the many easy trails in the vicinity: the Rotary Trail (3km/2 miles) is one of the most popular hikes, running from 7th Street to the confluence of the Fraser and Coquihalla rivers. Some 6km (4 miles) northeast of the town, the Coquihalla Canyon Provincial Park offers more trails and impressive views of the cliffs flanking the Coquihalla gorge.

One of the most dramatic stretches of the Fraser begins at the town of Yale, 25km (15.5 miles) north of Hope, the Fraser's navigable limit and a former Hudson's Bay Company trading post. During the gold rush of 1858 it became the largest town in North America west of Chicago and north of San Francisco, with a population of more than

20,000. Yale, like towns to the north such as Lytton, is a center for white-water rafting, though most people take a more sedate overview of the river and its canyon (here 180m/590ft deep) from the highway at Hell's Gate, 20km (12.5 miles) north of Yale, and the panoramic **Air-Tram** cable car across the gorge nearby.

✚ 135 D5

ℹ 919 Water Avenue, Hope ☎ 604/869-2021; www.hopebc.ca

Air-Tram

✉ Hell's Gate, Trans-Canada Hwy, Boston Bar, 28km (17 miles) north of Yale ☎ 604/867-9277; www.hellsgateairtram.com ⏱ Mid-May to early Sep daily 9:30–5:30; early Sep to mid-Oct, mid-Apr to mid-May daily 10–4 ✋ Moderate

GLACIER NATIONAL PARK

If you're coming from the west, Glacier National Park will provide a majestic foretaste of the Rockies beyond, and if you're coming from the Rockies, then Glacier's scenery will strike you as equally spectacular. Strictly speaking, Glacier protects part of the Selkirk and Columbia mountains, which are not part of the Rockies, though on the ground you will notice little difference, either in the quality of the landscapes or the manner in which they can be admired from the road – in this case the Trans-Canada Highway, which bisects the park by way of Rogers Pass (1,321m/4,334ft).

As the park's name suggests, glaciers – 422 of them – are the park's distinguishing feature, and 14 percent of the region is permanently cloaked in ice or snow: scientists have also identified 68 new glaciers forming on previously melted ice sheets, a rare

phenomenon. One of the largest, the still-growing Illecillewaet Glacier, is easily admired from the road.

Mount Dawson, at 3,390m (11,122ft) is the park's highest point, the ice and high terrain creating an often inhospitable environment. After immense hardships, the transcontinental railway was driven over the pass in 1885, but such were the problems with avalanches that a tunnel was bored under the pass in 1916. Until 1962, when the highway was built, the area remained all but inaccessible. The world's largest avalanche-control system is now required to keep the road open.

Stop at the Rogers Pass visitor center for more information on the park and some fascinating insights on how avalanches are managed. There are also more than 20 trails in the park (totaling 140km/87 miles), including some easy strolls from the highway, notably the Loop Trail (1.6km/1 mile), with lots of viewpoints, and the ten-minute Hemlock Grove Boardwalk. Most day hikes start at the Illecillewaet campsite, many of them offering excellent views of the glaciers, the Abbott's Ridge, Great Glacier and Avalanche Crest trails in particular.

➕ 137 B7

ℹ Rogers Pass Visitor Centre ☎ 250/837-6275 or 250/837-7500; www.pc.gc.ca/glacier ⏱ Mid-Jun to early Sep daily 8–7; Apr to mid-Jun, early Sep–Oct daily 9–5; Dec–Mar daily 7–5. Closed Nov. Hours may vary ✋ Park permit inexpensive ❓ Guided walks from the visitor center Jul–Aug

HIGHWAY 3

Highway 3 ambles across the most southerly part of British Columbia, shadowing Canada's border with the US. It's a strange road of mixed scenery, glorious in parts, drab in others, the best stretches coming in the section between Hope (► 90) and Keremeos. Travel this section and you'll be able to follow a perfect itinerary across the province, allowing you to combine it with an exploration of the Okanagan (► 101) – and thus the Kootenays (► 32–33) – which is easily reached from Keremeos.

From Hope the road climbs into the Coast and Cascade ranges and some glorious mountain scenery, reaching Manning Provincial Park – one of the few parks in this region – 64km (40 miles) east of Hope. If you have time, take the 15km (9-mile) scenic drive to Cascade Lookout and perhaps tackle one of several easy walks from the highway, notably the 20-minute Sumallo Grove loop, accessed 10km (6 miles) east of the park's western entrance.

The scenery is less exalted around Princeton, but picks up again as you approach Hedley, with a lovely picnic stop overlooking the Similkameen River at Bromley Rock Provincial Park, 21km (13 miles) east of Princeton. Hedley itself is a former gold-mining town, now little more than a single street at the heart of grand countryside. The small but interesting **Hedley Museum** (which also offers visitor information) has archive photographs and displays on the region's mining heritage.

At rustic little Keremeos, a quaint and highly recommended stopover, the landscape changes again, becoming far more pastoral, thanks to a balmy climate that provides one of the longest growing seasons in Canada. As a result, this is fruit and vegetable country, the town being cradled by lush orchards, its fertile, narrow plain surrounded by pretty hills and mountains. Roadside stands sell all manner of fruit in season, while the **St. Laszlo Vineyard,** 1km (0.6 miles) east of the town, offers tours and tastings.

www.env.gov.bc.ca/bcparks

www.similkameencountry.org

➕ 135 E6

Hedley Museum

✉ 712 Daly Street, Hedley ☎ 250/292 8422 🕐 Mid-May to Aug daily 9–5; Sep to mid-May Thu–Mon 9–4 💵 Donation

St. Laszlo Vineyard

✉ 2605 Hwy 3, Site 95, Comp 8, Keremeos, BC, V0X 1N0 ☎ 250/499-2856 🕐 Daily 9–9

NELSON

British Columbia has some of the world's most beautiful scenery, but its towns, with one or two exceptions, are often functional, modern places. The most notable exception is Nelson (population 10,000), the main town of the Kootenays (► 32–33) region in the southeast of the province. An attractive and easy-going place, it has a hilly lakeside setting and more than 350 pretty wooden "heritage" houses (the town was memorably used as the setting for Steve Martin's film *Roxanne*). Over the years it has attracted numerous artists and writers (more per head of population than anywhere else in Canada), creating a lively arts and cultural scene, and a civilized town with a close-knit sense of community. There is also a respected art college, a school of Chinese medicine and a **museum.**

The result is a place with lots of cafés, galleries, bookshops and vintage clothes stores, making its grid of tree-lined streets a pleasure to browse and explore. In summer, Artwalk links a hundred or so of the town's galleries and studios: you can obtain details from the visitor center, which also has pamphlets on walks and drives around the area's heritage buildings. Another walk, to Pulpit Rock (1 hour), offers a lovely view of the town from the north side of Kootenay Lake. In summer, the town also offers a farmers' market (Saturdays in Cottonwood Falls Park) and a restored streetcar that runs along the lakeshore.

Out of town, the lakes, mountains and scenic drives of the Kootenays are virtually on the doorstep. Don't miss Kokanee

Glacier Provincial Park, 35km (21.5 miles) northeast of the town, with many hiking trails, long and short: some of the best (notably to Kokanee Lake) start from the Gibson Lake parking area, one of the park's entry points.

➕ 137 F7

ℹ️ 225 Hall Street ☎ 250/352-3433 or 1-877/663-5706 🕐 Jun–Aug daily 8:30–6; Sep–May Mon–Fri 8:30–5

Nelson Museum

✉️ 502 Vernon Street ☎ 250/352-9813 🕐 Mon–Sat 9–5

a drive through the heart of British Columbia

This is one of countless scenic drives in Western Canada, and a route that links – assuming you are on a tour across the region – three of the key areas of central BC: the Okanagan, Kootenays and Cascade and Columbia mountains.

Start at Vernon, the northernmost of the main towns in the Okanagan (➤ 101). Take Hwy 6 east toward Lumby, Cherryville and Needles.

Out of Vernon the highway glides through sublime pastoral landscapes of orchards, meadows and low, tree-covered hills. Beyond the settlements of Lumby and Cherryville it climbs into the Monashee Mountains (www.monasheetourism.com), passing through empty countryside before cresting the Monashee Pass (1,198m/3,930ft) and dropping into the Coldstream Valley for the ferry crossing at Needles on Lower Arrow Lake.

Take the five-minute ferry crossing to tiny Fauquier, which has the only motel and restaurant in the area (Arrow Lake Motel, tel: 250/269-7622) and continue north on Hwy 6 for 57km (35 miles) to Nakusp. If you are short of time, continue north via the ferry crossing at Galena Bay to Revelstoke. If not, drive east to Kaslo on Hwy 6 via New Denver.

Lakeside Nakusp in the Kootenays (➤ 32–33) makes a delightful stop for food or an overnight stay, as does backwoods New Denver, 47km (30 miles) to the east, a former silver-mining town with another fine lakeside setting. The road between the two is a wonderful drive through majestic mountain scenery, only bettered by the drive from New Denver to Kaslo (➤ 32), one of the most scenic stretches of road in the province.

It is 150km (93 miles) from Kaslo to Revelstoke via Gerrard and Galena Bay, a wild and dramatic route along mostly gravel road, so be sure to have a full tank of gas. Revelstoke has plenty of accommodations and leaves you well placed to head east toward the Rockies on Hwy 1 via Glacier National Park (➤ 92–93).

Distance 300km/186 miles (460km/285 miles via Kaslo)
Time 1–3 days
Start point Vernon ✚ 136 C4
End point Revelstoke ✚ 137 B6
Overnight stop Nakusp

KAMLOOPS

Kamloop's position, 355km (220 miles) from Vancouver, on several major highways and close to the center of southern British Columbia, means that it is a town you are likely to pass through on any number of itineraries across the province. Its outskirts sprawl in all directions across bare, sun-baked brown hills and arid river plains, with plenty of inexpensive accommodations options if you wish to break your journey. The old town center is more appealing, home to a pair of small historical museums, galleries of contemporary art and the **Kamloops Heritage Railway,** which offers visitors a 70-minute steam-train ride in the summer months.

✚ 136 B3

🛈 1290 West Trans-Canada Hwy ☎ 250/374-3377; www. tourismkamloops.com

Kamloops Heritage Railway

✉ 510 Lorne Street ☎ 250/374-2141; www.kamrail.com 🕓 Departures Jul–Aug Fri–Mon 🖐 Moderate

KOOTENAYS

Best places to see, ➤ 32–33.

OKANAGAN

The Okanagan comes as a surprise after the forests and snow-dusted mountains of much of British Columbia. A region of lakes and low hills, its marked microclimate – with hot summers and mild winters – allows for the growing of grapes, peaches and other warm-weather fruit. As a result, this is a pretty, pastoral corner, at least in its rural hinterland, for the region's lakeside towns, and Kelowna in particular, are big, booming places, popular as summer resorts and with a bustle uncharacteristic of British Columbia. Many US and Canadian visitors come here to idle by the lakes in July and August, but the best times to visit are in spring, when the fruit trees are in blossom, or in autumn, when the leaves are turning and the grape harvest begins. The region's other towns, Vernon and Penticton, resemble Kelowna, with sprawling, unattractive suburbs but pretty, well-kept centers. Vernon is close to the region's key historic sight, the **O'Keefe Ranch,** a collection of historic buildings that vividly evoke 19th-century pioneer life. You could easily see much of the region passing through, or in a day or two's driving, preferably on the quieter roads on the western side of Lake Okanagan.

✚ 136 D3

ℹ 544 Harvey Avenue, Kelowna

☎ 250/861-1515; www.tourismkelowna.com

ℹ 533 Railway Street, Penticton

☎ 250/493-4055; www.tourismpenticton.ca

ℹ 701 Hwy 97, Vernon ☎ 250/542-1415; www.vernontourism.com

O'Keefe Ranch

✉ 12km (7.5 miles) north of Vernon, off Hwy 97 ☎ 250/542-7868; www.okeeferanch.ca 🕓 Jul–Aug daily 9–8; May, Jun, Sep to mid-Oct daily 9–5

✋ Moderate

SHUSWAP LAKE

Shuswap Lake comprises more than 1,000km (620 miles) of navigable waterways, part of an intermittently pretty corner of British Columbia between Kamloops to the west and the Monashee Mountains to the east. Most people drive along much of its length as they follow the Trans-Canada Highway. Its hinterland is filled with small provincial parks, crammed with fishing, hiking and other outdoor possibilities, but it is best known for the little town of Salmon Arm, 108km (67 miles) east of Kamloops. As its name suggests, this is a place associated with fish, for Shuswap Lake provides an important link in the Fraser and Thompson river systems, and is the most important salmon habitat in North America. In spawning season, in October, millions of fish pass through local rivers, attracting vast numbers of visitors who come to watch the spectacle.

🚩 137 B5

ℹ️ 200 Trans-Canada Highway, Salmon Arm ☎ 250/832-2230; www.csrd.bc.ca

WELLS GRAY PROVINCIAL PARK

Wells Gray is one of British Columbia's most enticing parks, on a scenic par with the better-known parks of the Canadian Rockies to the east. Its southern reaches are easily accessed from scenic Hwy 5 from Kamloops to Tête Jaune Cache (338km/210 miles) where you can pick up Hwy 16 east to Jasper, making the park a good stop off as part of a longer itinerary.

Drive north from Kamloops and you can access Sun Peaks Resort after 53km (33 miles), BC's second-largest winter sports destination after Whistler (it also offers plenty of hiking and other activities in the summer). Clearwater, 125km (77 miles) north of Kamloops, provides a good base for a day trip exploring the park, which is accessed from Hwy 5 via a 78km (48.5-mile) access road.

About 10km (6 miles) north of Clearwater on this road is Spahats Falls, one of several impressive waterfalls in the park. Just beyond the park entrance is a turnoff to Green Mountain Lookout, which provides a great viewpoint over a vast expanse of wilderness. Dawson Falls is the next major signposted sight, five minutes' walk from the road, followed by the trailhead for the Murtle River Trail (14km/8.7 miles), which offers more waterfalls. Close by is the turnoff for Helmcken Falls, the park's highlight, a cascade that, at 137m (450ft) high, is more than twice the height of Niagara Falls. Also see Ray Farm (1912), the picturesque former home of John Bunyon Ray, a former homesteader.

The park road ends at pretty Clearwater Lake, where you can rent canoes, camp or walk several easy short trails. Rafting trips on the Clearwater River can also be booked from several operators in Clearwater.

➕ 138 B4

ℹ Sun Peaks Resort ☎ 1-800/807-3257; www.sunpeaksresort.com

ℹ Hwy 5, Clearwater ☎ 250/674-2646; www.clearwaterbcchamber.com

WHISTLER

Whistler, the main focus of the 2010 Winter Olympic Games, is one of North America's premier recreational resorts. Set at the heart of the spectacular Coast Mountains, it lies within easy reach of Vancouver, just 125km (77 miles) to the south, connected by a major highway (Hwy 99) and with regular bus services from the city. Traditionally it has been seen as a winter sports resort, its activities centered on two mountains, Whistler and Blackcomb, with some of North America's longest, highest and most varied ski runs (suitable for all abilities), as well as boarding, sledging, snow-shoeing, dog-sled tours, snowmobiling and other activities.

More recently, however, it has emerged as a summer resort, with mountain-biking, in particular, a major activity. However, there are plenty of other activities, for all ages and abilities, and casual visitors can easily rent bicycles (and other outdoor equipment) in Whistler Village, the resort's purpose-built modern center. Hiking is excellent, with cable cars allowing walkers easy access to high-level trails. There are also four major golf courses locally (visit www.golfbc.com for more information), plus fishing, jet-boating and rafting, and a host of other activities. Visitor centers carry all the information you need to choose, book or pursue an activity.

www.tourismwhistler.com

www.whistlerchamber.com

www.whistlerblackcomb.com

✚ 134 B3

ℹ 4010 Whistler Way, Whistler Village Square

☎ 604/932-3928 or 1-888/869-2777.

Chamber of Commerce, 4230 Gateway Drive, Whistler Village

The Rockies

The Canadian Rockies are one of the world's great landscapes, a sublime medley of mountains, forests, lakes, rivers and glaciers that combines vast swathes of wilderness with almost limitless opportunities for hiking, mountain biking, fishing, winter sports and other outdoor activities.

Calgary □

The range stretches from the border with the United States almost to the Yukon in Canada's far north, straddling the provinces of Alberta and British Columbia, but the area most people visit is in the south, in the Rockies' four adjoining national parks: Banff and Jasper, the two largest, and Kootenay and Yoho, both much smaller, but with scenery that is every bit as impressive. Fantastic scenic roads run through all four parks, notably the Icefields Parkway between Banff and Jasper, but it's well worth tackling some of the region's many hikes – there's something for everyone, whatever your fitness levels – for a real taste of Canada's great outdoors.

BANFF

Banff is the gateway to Banff National Park (➤ 108–111) and the chief town of the four major parks of the Canadian Rockies. It's a busy, bustling place, especially in summer. Beautifully situated astride the Bow River, and in the shadow of the encircling mountains, it makes a pleasant stopover and an essential place for supplies if you're heading deeper into the park. If you're staying, be sure to book rooms well in advance, especially in summer.

The town provides a base for walks and drives in the park, though many people end up browsing the numerous souvenir and outdoor equipment stores in Banff Avenue, the main street. Cafés and good restaurants abound, and the excellent visitor center can point you to a handful of pleasant strolls in and around the town, as well as tour operators who run boating, fishing, riding and rafting trips. Bicycles can also be rented at several outlets.

The town also has three museums: the **Banff Park Museum,** with many stuffed animals indigenous to the park; the **Whyte Museum of the Canadian Rockies,** with displays devoted to the emergence of the Rockies as a tourist destination; and the **Luxton Museum,** home to rather dated displays related to the area's First Nations population. Many people pay a visit to the famous Banff Springs Hotel, and to the **Banff Gondola,** a busy cable car that offers excellent views. Also interesting is the **Cave and Basin National Historic Site,** discovered by three railway laborers in 1883. The reserve created around the hot springs there two years later was the germ of the present national

park. You can also bathe in the
Upper Hot Springs Pool.

✚ 141 F5

ℹ 224 Banff Avenue ☎ 403/762-2523;
www.pc.gc.ca/banff or
www.banfflakelouise.com 🕐 Late
Jun–Aug daily 8–8; mid-May to late
Jun, 1 Sep to mid-Sep 9–7; mid-Sep to
mid-May daily 9–5

Banff Park Museum

✉ 93 Banff Avenue ☎ 403/762-1558
🕐 Mid-May to Sep daily 10–6; Oct to
mid-May daily 1–5 ✋ Inexpensive

**Whyte Museum of the Canadian
Rockies**

✉ 111 Bear Street ☎ 403/762-2291;
www.whyte.org 🕐 Daily 10–5
✋ Inexpensive

Luxton Museum

✉ 1 Birch Avenue ☎ 403/762-2388; www.buffalonationsmuseum.ca
🕐 Daily 9–6 ✋ Inexpensive

Banff Gondola

✉ Mountain Avenue ☎ 403/762-5438; www.banffgondola.com 🕐 Jan
daily 10–4; Feb–Mar daily 10–5; Apr–May daily 8:30–6; Jun–Aug daily
7.30am–9pm; Sep to mid-Oct daily 8:30–6:30; mid-Oct to Nov daily 8:30–4:30;
Dec daily 10–4 ✋ Expensive

Cave and Basin National Historic Site

✉ Cave Avenue ☎ 403/762-1566 🕐 Mid-May to Sep daily 9–6; Oct to
mid-May Mon–Fri 11–4, Sat–Sun 9:30–5 ✋ Inexpensive ❓ Daily guided
tours at 11, 2 and 4 (Sat–Sun only at 11 Oct to mid-May)

Upper Hot Springs Pool

✉ Mountain Avenue ☎ 403/762-1515; www.hotsprings.ca 🕐 Mid-May to
early Sep daily 9am–11pm; early Sep to mid-May Sun–Thu 10–10, Fri–Sat
10am–11pm ✋ Moderate

BANFF NATIONAL PARK

Banff National Park is the best-known of the major parks protecting the Canadian Rockies. It began life in 1885 as a small reserve to protect natural hot springs near the present site of Banff, the park's major town (➤ 106–107). In 1887 this became the Rocky Mountains Park, Canada's first national park (and the world's second, after Yellowstone in the United States). The park had a practical as well as environmental purpose, being partly designed to lure visitors, and thus help pay for and promote the government-backed transcontinental railway.

To look at a map of the park today can give the impression that this is a relatively populated area. In fact, there is only one town worthy of the name (Banff), plus Lake Louise (➤ 122–123), a small, modern village and resort 58km (36 miles) north of Banff, to which it is linked by two highways: the Trans-Canada (Hwy 1) and the specially built scenic Bow Valley Parkway. Canmore, just outside the park to the south, is a fast-developing town (➤ 113), but less attractive as a base than Banff or Lake Louise.

A major road, the sublime Icefields Parkway (➤ 30–31), links Lake Louise to Jasper, while the Trans-Canada Highway runs west from Lake Louise to Yoho National Park (➤ 126–128) and Hwy 93 leaves the Trans-Canada Highway midway between Banff and Lake Louise to run through Kootenay National Park (➤ 118–119).

To get the best out of the park, allow at least three days, depending on how keen you are to tackle a hike – there are more than 1,500km (930 miles) of trails to suit all abilities – or pursue other outdoor activities such as biking, riding or golf. The visitor centers at Banff and Lake Louise carry details of all hikes, but the most popular trails can be busy: most of the trailheads (the point from which hikes start) are on the Trans-Canada Highway or Bow Valley Parkways north and south of Banff.

The best easy strolls close to Banff town are Bow Falls Trail (2.4km/1.5 miles), the Hoodoos Trail (10.2km/6.5 miles), Marsh Loop Trail (2.5km/1.5 miles) and Sundance Canyon trail (2km/1.25

miles): distances are round-trip. Standout day hikes are Cory Pass Trail (5.8km/3.6 miles), which involves a tough 915m/3,000ft ascent, but has wonderful views, and Cascade Amphitheatre (13.2km/8 miles, 610m/2,000ft ascent). There are also five major trails off the Bow Valley Parkway, of which the best short walk is the Johnston Canyon Trail (7.4km/4.6 miles, 520m/1,705ft ascent) and the best day hike the Rockbound Lake Trail (16.8km/10.4 miles, 760m/2,493ft ascent). The outstanding walk off Hwy 1 between Banff and Lake Louise is to Bourgeau Lake (15km/9.3 miles, 725m/2,378ft ascent).

Spend one day in and around Banff, which is an obvious base (► 106–107); one (or two) hiking or perhaps rafting on Banff's Bow River, which offers gentle family-friendly trips (more extreme

white-water outings are available on rivers such as Kicking Horse in neighboring Yoho, to which operators will transport you from Banff); and one day perhaps visiting Lake Minnewanka, 10km (6 miles) northeast of Banff, the park's largest lake, where you can take 90-minute **boat tours** and walk or picnic on the banks.

You may then wish to spend a day or two in Lake Louise or Moraine Lake (➤ 34–35), perhaps with excursions into Kootenay National Park (➤ 118–119), and one day driving the Icefields Parkway (➤ 30–31).

➕ 141 E5 ℹ️ Banff (➤ 107), Lake Louise (➤ 123)

Lake Minnewanka Boat Tours

☎ 403/762-3473; www.minnewankaboattours.com 🕐 Mid-May to Sep daily 4–5 tours 💷 Expensive

CALGARY

Many visitors come to Calgary expecting to do little but pass through on their way to the Rockies – Banff is just 90 minutes' drive away. In the event, most people find this a fine city, built on revenues from oil and cattle, its glittering downtown skyscrapers rising from the undulating Albertan prairie, its museums and attractive downtown streets – edged by the ice-clear Bow River – well worth a day or more of sightseeing.

Gain an overview of the city, as well as a fantastic view of the Rockies stretched across the western horizon, from the 190m (623ft) **Calgary Tower,** completed in 1968. Also leave plenty of time to wander the shops, cafés and restaurants of 7th Avenue SW and the Eau Claire Market by the river, as well as exploring **Calgary Zoo** (Canada's largest) and **Fort Calgary Historic Park,** site of a stockade built in 1875 to control lawlessness in Canada's pioneer country. Devote most time, however, to the modern **Glenbow Museum,** full of excellent art, and historical and First Nations displays. It's one of western Canada's best museums, second only to Victoria's Royal BC Museum.

🔹 141 F8

🔹 200–238 11th Avenue SE ☎ 403/263-8510 or 1-800/661-1678; www.tourismcalgary.com 🕒 Mon–Fri 8–5

Calgary Tower

✉ Corner of Centre Street and 9th Avenue SW ☎ 403/266-7171; www.calgarytower.com 🕐 Hours vary seasonally: call for latest details ✋ Moderate

Calgary Zoo

✉ 1300 Zoo Road NE ☎ 403/232-9300 or 1-800/588-9993; www.calgaryzoo.org 🕐 Daily 9–6 (last entry 5) 💲 Expensive

Fort Calgary Historic Park

✉ 750-9th Ave SE ☎ 403/290-1875; www.fortcalgary.com 🕐 Daily 9–5 ✋ Moderate

Glenbow Museum

✉ 130-9th Avenue SW ☎ 403/268-4100; www.glenbow.org 🕐 Fri–Wed 9–5, Thu 9–9 ✋ Moderate

CANMORE AND KANANASKIS COUNTRY

Kananaskis Country is the name given to a group of beautiful provincial mountain parks between Calgary and Banff, partly designed to take some of the pressure off Banff National Park. Popular with locals, the area has excellent hiking and other outdoor activities, plus superb winter sports at Nakiska and Fortress Mountain. Much of the region is accessed via Hwy 40 (off Hwy 1), though one of the busiest areas now centers on Canmore, 28km (17 miles) from Banff. This booming town has fewer restrictions on development than its near neighbor and, while not as beautifully situated, makes a good base, with plenty of accommodations and innumerable opportunities for outdoor activities.

✚ 141 F6

ℹ 2801 Bow Valley Trail, Canmore ☎ 403/678-5277 or 1-800/ 661-8888; www.discoveralberta. com, www.skinakiska.com, www.skifortress.com 🕐 Jun–Aug daily 8–8; Sep–May daily 9–6

ICEFIELDS PARKWAY

Best places to see, ➤ 30–31.

JASPER

Much as Banff is virtually the only center in Banff National park, so Jasper, 287km (178 miles) north of Banff, is the only town in Jasper National Park (➤ 116–117). But where Banff has all the trappings of a modern town, more modest Jasper still preserves something of the gritty, windswept charm of a frontier settlement. It is, though, an excellent base, albeit one that is less spectacularly situated than its southern counterpart.

Like Banff, it owes its existence largely to the railway. First Nations peoples had used the Yellowhead Pass to the west across the mountains for centuries, and trappers and traders had established outposts from about 1810 onward. But it was the arrival in 1911 of the Grand Trunk Pacific Railway, the country's second transcontinental railway, that led first to the formation of a tent city for workers and, eventually, a permanent settlement.

Today, the railway (plus Hwy 16) still runs through the heart of the town, which collects along two main thoroughfares, Connaught Drive and Patricia Street. These streets contain plenty of cafés, restaurants and stores, but also the main park visitor center and the offices of several tour operators who will organize hiking and other outdoor activities in and around the town, and in the park at large. In particular, Jasper is a major rafting base, with a wide range of trips on the local Athabasca river.

Otherwise the town has little in the way of obvious attractions, save the small **Yellowhead Museum & Archives,** with displays devoted to the fur trade and the coming of the railway. The most obvious excursion is the **Jasper Tramway,** 7km (4 miles) south of the center, Canada's longest and highest cable car. The car leaves you at a viewpoint and restaurant at 2,285m (7,495ft), with sweeping views and the opportunity to follow an obvious trail (make sure you have suitable clothing and footwear) to the summit of Whistlers Mountain (2,470m/8,104ft).

Also popular are Pyramid and Patricia lakes just north of the town, with lots of easy hiking and picnicking opportunities, plus trips to Maligne Canyon and Maligne Lake (➤ 116–117).

➕ 140 A3

ℹ 500 Connaught Drive ☎ 780/852-6176; www.pc.gc.ca/jasper

🕐 Jun–Sep daily 9–7; Oct–May daily 9–4

Yellowhead Museum & Archives

✉ 400 Pyramid Lake Road ☎ 780/852-3013; www.jaspermuseum.org

🕐 May–Sep daily 10–5; Oct–Apr Tue–Sun 10–5 ✋ Inexpensive

Jasper Tramway

✉ Whistlers Mountain Road ☎ 866/850-8726; www.jaspertramway.com

🕐 Mid-Apr to mid-May, late Aug to mid-Oct daily 10–5; mid-May to late Jun daily 9:30–6:30; late Jun–late Aug daily 9–8. Adverse weather may cause hours to vary ✋ Expensive

JASPER NATIONAL PARK

Jasper National Park tends to be overshadowed by Banff National Park to the south, but it covers a larger and wilder protected area, and is less busy and less commercialized. For keen hikers and campers, the backcountry is more extensive than Banff, with more long-distance trails. And for those who wish to escape some of Banff and Lake Louise's crowds, much of the park has a greater sense of wilderness.

Casual visitors should not be put off, however, for there are plenty of easy trails and manageable day hikes, as well as ways to enjoy the scenery without donning hiking boots. The most obvious is the Icefields Parkway (➤ 30–31), shared with Banff National Park (about half of the road's 230km/143 miles are in the Jasper park), along with scenic roads such as Hwy 16, which runs to the Yellowhead Pass (1,131m/3,711ft), 20km (12.5 miles) west of Jasper town, and then on to Mount Robson Provincial Park (➤ 124). You might also consider taking the majestic VIA Rail (www.viarail.ca) train ride from Jasper to Prince George.

Otherwise, the most popular excursion is a **lake cruise on Maligne Lake,** 48km (30 miles) southwest of Jasper via Maligne Lake Road (companies run tours and shuttle buses along the road if you are without your own transportation). The Rockies' largest natural lake (at 22km/13.5 miles long), Maligne Lake is staggeringly beautiful, and near the lakeshore it's possible to fish, ride and raft, or to rent canoes and row-boats. There are also a couple of easy trails on the east shore of the lake and to the

Schaffer viewpoint (3km/2 miles round-trip). One of the park's best day walks, the Opal Hills Circuit (8.2km/5 miles round-trip, 460m/1,509ft ascent) starts here, from the upper parking area.

En route to or from the lake, you might also explore Maligne Canyon (11km/7 miles from Jasper), a modest but often crowded canyon with short, easy trails. For other walks (including modest strolls), contact the Jasper visitor center: two of the best are Cavell Meadows (3.8km/2.4 miles one-way, 370m/1,213ft ascent), which starts 26km (16 miles) from Jasper town, and the harder Sulphur Skyline (4km/2.5 miles one-way, 700m/2,296ft ascent) from **Miette Hot Springs** (where you can bathe), 55km (34 miles) east of Jasper Town off Hwy 16.
➕ 140 C4

ℹ️ 500 Connaught Drive, Jasper ☎ 780/852-6176; www.pc.gc.ca/jasper

🕐 Apr to mid-Jun, Oct daily 9–5; mid-Jun to Aug daily 8:30–7; Sep daily 9–6; Nov–Mar daily 9–4

Maligne Lake Cruises

✉️ Maligne Tours, 627 Patricia Street, Jasper ☎ 780/852-3370; www.malignelake.com, www.mra.ab.ca 🕐 Departures hourly: ice melt–Jun 4 daily 10–3; Jun 5–24, Sep 4–end of season daily 10–4; Jun 25–Sep 3 daily 10–5 ✋ Expensive

Miette Hot Springs

✉️ Miette Road, off Hwy 16, 61km (38 miles) east of Jasper ☎ 780/866-3939 or 1-800/767-1611 🕐 Early May to mid-Jun, Sep to mid-Oct daily 10:30–9; mid-Jun to Aug 8:30am–10:30pm. Closed rest of year

KOOTENAY NATIONAL PARK

Kootenay is the least known of the four major national parks in the Canadian Rockies, and the one most often missed by visitors, many of whom prefer to follow Hwy 1 into Yoho or push on to Jasper along the Icefields Parkway. But not only is it well worth seeing, it is easily visited, a day being sufficient to drive the 200km (124 miles) there and back through the park along Hwy 93 from Castle Junction to Radium Hot Springs. It is a road that offers magnificent views and several hikes, long and short, from trailheads along the way.

The highway climbs quickly from Castle Junction to Vermilion Pass (1,637m/5,370ft), the border with British Columbia and the Continental Divide, the division between the watersheds of rivers that flow to the Atlantic and those that flow to the Arctic or Pacific oceans. Here is the short Fireweed Trail (2km/1.25 miles) into the forest and, 3km (2 miles) beyond, the Stanley Glacier Trail (8.4km/5.2 miles, 365m/1,197ft ascent) for views of the eponymous glacier. Much easier is the stroll along Marble Canyon (0.8km/0.5 miles), 8km (5 miles) from Vermilion Pass, and the nearby walk to the Paint Pots, fascinating old ocher beds once used by the area's earliest inhabitants.

Vermilion Crossing, 20km (12.5 miles) beyond the Paint Pots Trail, is a tiny settlement and the only place to find lodgings, food and fuel in the park. It also has a visitor center and is the start point of several trails. After Kootenay Crossing – a ceremonial spot where the ribbon opening Hwy 93 was cut in 1923 – the road begins to climb, culminating in the Kootenay Valley Viewpoint, with superlative vistas of the Mitchell and Vermilion mountains.

Thereafter, the road drops through Sinclair Canyon toward **Radium Hot Springs,** a sprawling town that takes its name from the park-run natural hot springs (open to the public) on Hwy 93 in the shadow of the canyon.

➕ 141 F5

ℹ️ 7556 Main Street East, Radium Hot Springs ☎ 250/347-9505; www. pc.gc.ca/kootenay 🕐 Mid-May to mid-Jun, Sep 1 to mid-Sep daily 9–5;

mid-Jun to Aug daily 9–7; mid-Sep to mid-Oct daily 9–4. Closed rest of year

ℹ️ Kootenay Park Lodge, Vermilion Crossing ☎ 403/762 9196; www. kootenayparklodge.com 🕐 Mid-May to Jun, Sep–early Oct daily 10–5; Jul–Aug daily 9–6. Closed rest of year

Radium Hot Springs

✉️ Hwy 93 ☎ 250/347-9485 or 1 800/767-1611; www.hotsprings.ca 🕐 Mid-May to mid-Jun, early Sep to mid-Sep daily 9–5; mid-Jun to early Sep 9–7; mid-Sep to mid-Oct 9–4 ♿ Inexpensive

a drive along the Bow Valley Parkway

Instead of taking Hwy 1 between Banff and Lake Louise, take the parallel Bow Valley Parkway, a specially built scenic road with many points of interest and easy hikes. Drive early to avoid crowds on the trails and for the best chance of seeing wildlife.

Drive west from Banff on Hwy 1 and after 5km (3 miles) take the Bow Valley Parkway exit.

After 3km (2 miles) the Backswamp Lookout offers mountain views and the chance to spot wildlife, including bighorn sheep, beaver, muskrat, osprey and mountain goat. Drive another 3km (2 miles) to the Muleshoe Picnic Area and learn about the park authority's controlled forest-burning program.

After 18km (11 miles) is the trailhead for the easy Johnston Canyon Trail (2.7km/1.7 miles one way).

This is a spectacular but busy trail along a canyon to a pair of impressive waterfalls. Another 3km (2 miles) beyond is Moose Meadows, where you may see grazing elk.

Drive another 5km (3 miles) west and look out for a panel marking the site of Silver City.

Silver City was a shanty town that filled with 3,000 silver miners in 1883, though there never was any silver – unscrupulous local businessmen had started a rumor to make money from prospectors.

After 24km (15 miles) you come to Castle Mountain Junction, with a café, store and fuel station. Drive another 5km (3 miles) past the Rockbound Lake trailhead (8.4km/5.2 miles one-way), Castle Cliffs Viewpoint and Castle Crags trailhead.

This last trail (3.7km/2.3 miles, 520m/1,705ft ascent) is short but steep, climbing above the tree line to offer fine views of the Bow Valley and mountains beyond.

Drive on past Baker Creek to Morant's Curve, about 5km (3 miles) east of Lake Louise. Continue to the end of the Parkway at the Lake Louise Gondola and continue to Lake Louise Village.

Morant's Curve is one of the Rockies' most famous viewpoints, thanks to a panorama that embraces the railway and a broad sweep of the mountains.

Distance 52km (32 miles)
Time 1–5 hours depending on stops and hikes
Start point Banff ✚ 141 F5
End point Lake Louise ✚ 137 E5
Lunch Baker Creek Bistro or Lake Louise Village
🔢 Banff (➤ 107), Lake Louise (➤ 123)

LAKE LOUISE

Lake Louise is the second center in Banff National Park
after Banff, and divides into two parts. Just off the main
Hwy 1 is Lake Louise Village, a small purpose-built area
comprising a handful of shops, park visitor center, hotels,
a youth hostel and cafés. From here, Lake Louise Drive
winds 4.5km (2.8 miles) and climbs 200m (655ft) to Lake
Louise, one of the most famous sights in the Rockies. On
the lakeshore stands the Chateau Lake Louise hotel, a
vast high-rise that anywhere else might be a blight on the
landscape, but which here is dwarfed by the extraordinary
grandeur of the lake and its forest and glacier-hung

mountains. The lakefront is invariably extremely busy, so visit early if possible. Easy trails follow the lake shore, or you can climb to Lake Agnes (where there is a Teahouse for refreshments), a very popular 3.4km (2-mile) walk with 300m (984ft) of ascent.

This can be combined with other trails to reach the head of the valley above the lake. You can also rent canoes to take on the lake. Across the Bow Valley, a short way northeast of Lake Louise Village, is the **Lake Louise Gondola,** a cable car that runs to a superb viewpoint at 2,088m (6,850ft).

➕ 141 E5

ℹ️ Lake Louise Village ☎ 403/522-3833; www.pc.gc.ca 🕐 Jan–Apr, Oct–Dec daily 9–4; May to mid-Jun and Sep 14–30 daily 9–5; mid-Jun to early Sep daily 9–8; early Sep–Sep 13 daily 9–7

Lake Louise Gondola

☎ 403/522-3555 or 1-800/258-7669; www.lakelouisegondola.com
🕐 Mid-May to mid-Jun, early Sep–Sep 30 daily 9–4:30; mid-Jun to early Sep daily 9–5 ✋ Expensive

MORAINE LAKE

Best places to see, ➤ 34–35.

MOUNT ROBSON

Mount Robson is the highest point in the Canadian Rockies (3,954m/12,973ft), and is protected by a provincial park that borders Jasper National Park to the west. One of the mountain's many beauties is that in good weather its colossal outlines can be seen from the road, Hwy 16, which runs from Jasper, about 60km (37 miles) to the east. In the first 24km (15 miles) of highway from Jasper, to the border of British Columbia and the Mount Robson Provincial Park, the road (shadowed by the railway) climbs to the Yellowhead Pass (1,131m/3,711ft). If the scenery here seems relatively tame, the view of Mount Robson, when it comes, is breathtaking, partly because the mountain stands in isolation, and partly because its monumental south face – a sheer rise of some 3,100m (10,171ft) – presents itself to the viewer (pick a clear day for your trip). There is a seasonal visitor center near the viewpoint, plus a café and garage nearby, but very few other facilities, so stock up in Jasper. You can return to Jasper, or continue south or west on highways 5 or 16, both extremely scenic drives.

✚ 139 B6 (off map)

🛈 Hwy 16 ☎ 250/566-4325; www.elp.gov.bc.ca/bcparks 🕐 Jun, Sep daily 8–5; Jul–Aug daily 8–8. Closed rest of the year

WATERTON LAKES NATIONAL PARK

Waterton is the Cinderella of the Rockies' national parks, but only because it occupies a region close to the US border that is difficult to incorporate on any logical tour of Alberta and British Columbia. On the ground, the mountain scenery, the hiking (with 255km/ 158 miles of excellent trails) and other outdoor activities are just as good as in the four better-known parks to the north. The park, which dates from 1895, centers on the small town of Waterton, prettily situated on the shores of Upper Waterton Lake. Waterton contains most of the park's accommodations, services and tours, with lots of hiking from, or close to the town, plus boat trips on the lake. Two scenic roads run west from Waterton into the heart of the park, the Akamina Parkway, which leads 20km

(12.5 miles) to Cameron Lake (walk back to Waterton on the sublime Carthew-Alderson Trail: 19km/11.8 miles, 612m/2,007ft ascent), and the Red Rock Canyon Parkway, which runs 15km (9.3 miles) to the mouth of the eponymous canyon.

✚ 141 F6 (off map)

🛈 Entrance Road ☎ 403/859-5133; www.pc.gc.ca/watertonlakes ◉ Early May–early Oct daily 8–7

YOHO NATIONAL PARK

Yoho takes its name from a Cree First Nations word meaning "wonder," testament to the majesty of the scenery in a national park many believe is the superior of both its neighbors, Banff and Jasper. Much smaller than these more famous parks, it lies wholly in British Columbia, bisected by the Trans-Canada Highway (Hwy 1) and home to just one village, Field, 28km (17.5 miles) west of Lake Louise.

The presence of the road makes it easy to breeze through the park admiring the scenery from a car or bus (the railway also shadows the road, but it no longer carries public services). As ever, though, it is well worth lingering, perhaps spending the day here before returning to Lake Louise or Banff, where there are far more accommodations options.

Two side roads north from the Trans-Canada offer access to the park's interior. The first leaves the highway about 3km (1.8 miles) east of Field, just after the Lower Spiral Tunnel Lookout, a viewpoint that offers views of the exits and entrances to the railway's famous Spiral Tunnels. These are two figure-of-eight galleries built in the 1880s to help the line negotiate the region's 4 percent gradients, then the steepest of any commercial railway in North America. Time it right and you can see the last box cars of freight trains entering a tunnel as their locomotive emerges close by.

The side road runs 9km (5.6 miles) up the Yoho Valley, coming to a dead end near Takkakaw Falls, one of the park's highlights. Taking their name from the Cree word for "magnificent," the falls are 245m (804ft) high, making them one of Canada's highest waterfalls (Niagara Falls are 52m/170ft high). Several hiking trails leave from the waterfalls' parking area, including the easy Point Lace Falls (1.9km/1.2 miles one-way, minimum ascent) and Laughing Falls (3.8km/2.3 miles, 60m/197ft ascent). Also extremely popular is the Twin Falls Trail (8.5km/5.3 miles one-way, 290m/951ft ascent).

The Yoho Pass trail (10.9km/6.7 miles, 310m/1,017ft ascent, 510m/1,673ft descent) crosses west and drops down to Emerald Lake, which can also be reached by the second of the side roads off the Trans-Canada, 2km (1.2 miles) west of Field. This is home to the Emerald Lake Lodge, one of the Rockies' premier hotels, as well as a network of trails, including an easy (and wheelchair-accessible) nature trail (4.6km/2.8 miles round trip), Hamilton Falls (1.6km/1 mile round trip) and Hamilton Lake (5.5km/3.4 miles one-way, 850m/2,788ft ascent).

A third area, Lake O'Hara, can also be approached by road, but here there are stringent quota systems (apply online or to the visitor center for details), making casual visits difficult.

Field and the Burgess Shales

The tiny village of Field began life as a railway construction camp in 1884. It has guesthouses, a park visitor center and a hotel. It is also the base for guided tours of the **Burgess Shales,** a UNESCO World Heritage Site. The shales are layers of sedimentary rock riddled with the fossils of 120 types of soft-bodied creatures from the Middle Cambrian period (515–530 million years ago), one of only three places in the world where such fossils are found. Note that tours must be pre-booked and involve quite tough climbs of over 700m (2,300ft).

✚ 140 E4

ℹ Hwy 1, Field ✉ 250/343-6783; www.pc.gc.ca/yoho ⓦ Jan–Apr, late Sep–Dec daily 9–4; May to mid-Jun, Sep 1–late Sep daily 9–5; mid-Jun to Aug daily 9–7

Yoho-Burgess Shale Foundation

☎ 1/800/343-3006 (Mon–Fri 10–3); www.burgess-shale.bc.ca ⓦ Guided tours Jul to mid-Sep

Index

Acknowledgments

The Automobile Association would like to thank the following photographers, companies and picture libraries for their assistance in the preparation of this book.

Abbreviations for the picture credits are as follows: (t) top; (b) bottom; (l) left; (r) right; (c) centre; (AA) AA World Travel Library.

4l Float plane, AA/J Tims; **4c** Butchart Gardens, AA/C Sawyer; **4r** Canada Place, AA/C Sawyer; **5l** Rosemary Rock, AA/J Tims; **5c** Kits beach, AA/J Tims; **6/7** Float plane, AA/J Tims; **10/11** Chinese New Year, AA; **13t** West Vancouver Bus, AA/M Dent; **13b** Sky Train, AA/J Tims; **20/21** Butchart Gardens, AA/C Sawyer; **22/23** Butchart Gardens, AA/J Tims; **23tc** Dahlia in Butchart Gardens, AA/C Sawyer; **23tr** Fountain in Butchart Gardens, AA/J Tims; **24** Canada Place, AA/C Sawyer; **24/25** Canada Place, AA/J Tims; **26t** Granville Island market, AA/J Tims; **26c** Granville Island gull, AA/J Tims; **26b** Granville Island, AA/J Tims; **27** Granville Island, AA/J Tims; **28/29** Grouse Mountain, AA/P Timmermans; **29** Grouse Mountain bear statue, AA/J Tims; **30/31** Banff National Park Bow Lake, AA/J Tims; **31t** View from Icefields Parkway, AA/P Bennett; **31c** Jasper National Park Parker Ridge Trek AA/J Tims; **32/33** Kootenay Lake, AA/C Sawyer; **33** Chipmunk in Marble Canyon, AA/J Tims; **34/35** Moraine Lake, AA/C Sawyer; **35c** Canoeing on Moraine Lake, AA/J Tims; **35b** Banff National Park Moraine Lake, AA/J Tims; **36** Museum of Anthropology statues, AA/J Tims; **37t** Museum of Anthropology, AA/J Tims; **37b** First Nation textile in Museum of Anthropology, AA/P Bennett; **38/39t** Royal British Columbia Museum, AA/J Tims; **38/39b** Totem poles in Royal British Columbia Museum, AA/J Tims; **39** Totem poles at Royal British Columbia Museum AA/M Dent; **40** Stanley Park Flower Garden, AA/J Tims; **40/41** City from Stanley Park, AA/P Bennett; **42/43** Canada Place, AA/C Sawyer; **46** Capilano Suspension Bridge, AA/J Tims; **47l** Salmon Hatchery Capilano River Regional Park, AA/J Tims; **47r** Capilano Suspension Bridge, AA/J Tims; **48** Dr Sun Yat Sen Gardens, AA/J Tims; **49** Chinatown Night Market, AA/J Tims; **50** Coal Harbour, AA/J Tims; **51** Inuit sculpture at English Bay, AA/P Timmermans; **52** Gastown shops, AA/J Tims; **53** Steam clock in Gastown, AA/J Tims; **54/55t** Boat off Galiano Island, AA/J Tims; **54/55b** Ferry off Galiano Island, AA/J Tims; **56** Vancouver Museum, AA/J Tims; **57** Lighthouse Park, AA/J Tims; **58/59** City seen from Lonsdale Quay, AA/J Tims; **59** Lynn Canyon Park waterfall, AA/J Tims; **60** Marine Building, AA/J Tims; **61** View to Mount Baker AA/P Bennett; **62/63** Queen Elizabeth Park, AA/J Tims; **64** Science World, AA/J Tims; **65t** Vancouver Aquarium, AA/J Tims; **65b** Whale in Vancouver Aquarium, AA/C Sawyer; **66c** Emily Carr's Rhythm of Nature in Vancouver Art Gallery, AA/C Sawyer; **66b** Emily Carr landscape in Vancouver Art Gallery, AA/C Coe; **67** View from Harbour Center AA/J Tims; **68** Maritime Museum Heritage Harbour, AA/J Tims; **69** Vancouver Public Library, AA/J Tims; **71** Coal Harbour, AA/J Tims; **72** Sakana Bistro in Yaletown, AA/J Tims; **73** Float plane, AA/J Tims; **74** Art Gallery of Greater Victoria, AA/J Tims; **75** Beacon Hill Park, AA/J Tims; **77** Market Square, AA/P Bennett; **78** Craigdarroch Castle, AA/J Tims; **79** Helmcken House, AA/J Tims; **80/81** Empress Hotel, AA/J Tims; **82** Lighthouse lamp at Maritime Museum, AA/J Tims; **83** Old Town in Victoria, AA/J Tims; **84** Parliament Buildings, AA/P Timmermans; **85** Parliament Buildings, AA/J Tims; **86c** Point Ellice House and Gardens, Ceara Lorie Point Ellice House and Gardens National Historic Site; **86b** Point Ellice House and Gardens, Ceara Lorie Point Ellice House and Gardens National Historic Site; **87** Whale watching with Prince of Whales off Vancouver Island, AA/J Tims; **88** Whale watching with Price of Whales off Vancouver Island, AA/C Sawyer; **89** Lake Okanagan marina, AA/C Sawyer; **90/91** Fraser Canyon, AA/J Tims; **91** Fraser Canyon Hell's Gate Airtram, AA/J Tims; **92/93** View from Abbott Ridge in Glacier National Park, Kurt Werby/Getty Images; **94** View from Highway 3, AA/J Tims; **94/95** View from Highway 3, AA/J Tims; **96/97** View from Gyro Park Nelson, Photolibrary Group; **98/99** Mount Revelstone National Park Mount Balsam, AA/J Tims; **100/101** Kamloops Lake, Kelly Funk/Getty Images; **101** Horses in Okanagan, AA/J Tims; **102/103** Salmon Arm on Shuswap Lake, AA/J Tims; **103** Wells Gray Provincial Park, AA/J Tims; **104** Whistler chairlift, AA/P Bennett; **105** Yoho National Park Emerald Lake, AA/J Tims; **106** Banff town, AA/J Tims; **107** Banff train station, AA/J Tims; **109** Banff National Park Peyto Lake, AA/J Tims; **110/111** Banff National Park Lake Louise, AA/J Tims; **111** Banff National Park Lake Minnewanka, AA/J Tims; **112** Calgary, AA/P Bennett; **113** Canmore, AA/J Tims; **114** Jasper town, AA/J Tims; **115** Jasper town, AA/J Tims; **116/117** Jasper National Park Patricia Lake, AA/J Tims; **118** Kootenay National Park Vermillion River, AA/J Tims; **119** Kootenay National Park wildflowers, AA/J Tims; **120/121** Banff National Park along Bow Valley Parkway, AA/P Bennett; **122/123** Banff National Park Lake Louise, AA/J Tims; **124** Mount Robson, AA/C Sawyer; **125t** Waterton Lakes National Park Cameron Lake, AA/P Bennett; **125b** Waterton Lakes National Park Buffalo, AA/J Tims; **127** Yoho National Park Emerald Lake, AA/J Tims; **129** Jasper National Park Athabasca Glacier, AA/P Bennett

Every effort has been made to trace the copyright holders, and we apologise in advance for any accidental errors. We would be happy to apply any corrections in the following edition of this publication.

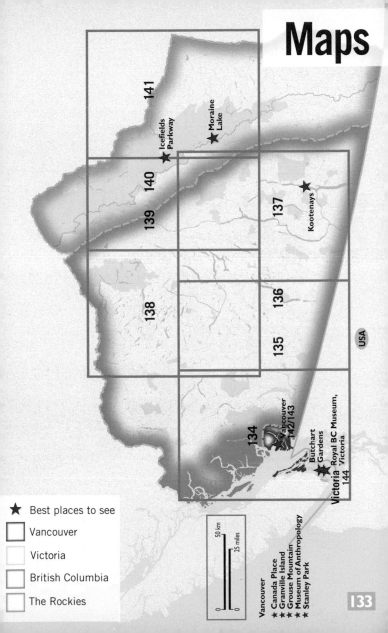

Maps

141

Icefields Parkway ★

★ Moraine Lake

140

139

★ Kootenays

137

138

136

135

USA

134

Vancouver 142/143

Butchart Gardens

Victoria – Royal BC Museum, Victoria

★ Best places to see

☐ Vancouver

☐ Victoria

☐ British Columbia

☐ The Rockies

50 km

25 miles

0

Vancouver
★ Canada Place
★ Granville Island
★ Grouse Mountain
★ Museum of Anthropology
★ Stanley Park

133

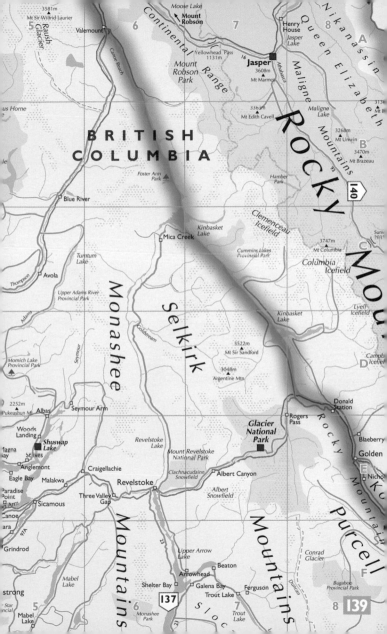

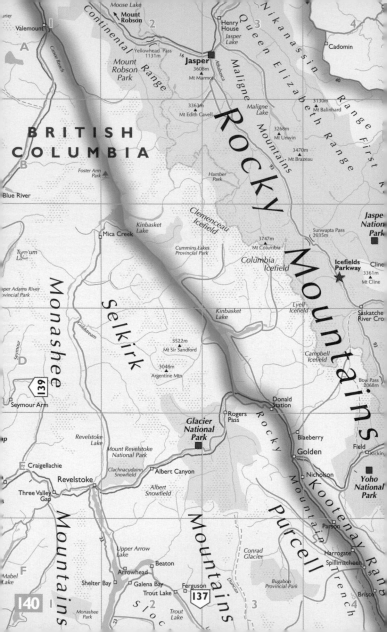

Moose Lake

Mount Robson 2

Valemount

Continental Range

Yellowhead Pass
1131m

Mount Robson Park

Jasper
3608m
Mt Marmot

Henry House 3

Jasper Lake

Queen Elizabeth Range

Nikanassin Range

Cadomin

4

40

First R

BRITISH
COLUMBIA

Blue River

Foster Arm Park

3363m
Mt Edith Cavell

Maligne Lake

Maligne Mountains

3130m
Mt Balinhard

3268m
Mt Unwin

3470m
Mt Brazeau

Hamber Park

Clemenceau Icefield

Cummins Lakes Provincial Park

Columbia Icefield

3747m
Mt Columbia

Sunwapta Pass 2035m

Jasper National Park

Icefields Parkway

Cline

3361m
Mt Cline

ROCKY Mountains

Mica Creek

Kinbasket Lake

Tum um Lake

per Adams River ovincial Park

Coldstream

Selkirk

Monashee

Kinbasket Lake

Lyell Icefield

Saskatche River Cro

93

3522m
Mt Sir Sandford

3048m
Argentine Mtn

Campbell Icefield

Bow Pass 2068m

Seymour

139

Seymour Arm

Donald Station

Rogers Pass

Glacier National Park

Revelstoke Lake

Mount Revelstoke National Park

Clachnacudainn Snowfield

Albert Canyon

Blaeberry

Golden

Nicholson

Field

Yoho National Park

Rocky Mountain

Craigellachie

Revelstoke

Albert Snowfield

Three Valley Gap

Upper Arrow Lake

Beaton

Arrowhead

Mabel Lake

Shelter Bay

Galena Bay

Ferguson

137

Trout Lake

Conrad Glacier

Duncan

Bugaboo Provincial Park

Purcell Mountains

Parson

Harrogate

Spillimacheen

Brisc

Kootenay Rang

Rocky Mountain Trench

Monashee Mountains

Monashee Park

Sloc

Trout Lake

ALBERTA

Pembina

Wabamun Lake
627

A

Brazeau

North Saskatchewan

Alsike

Breton

Brazeau Lake

Buck Lake

Alder Flats

Buck Lake

Winfield

13

Westerose

B

Bighorn Range

Nordegg
11

North Saskatchewan

Abraham Lake
752

337m
Michener

Crimson Lake Provincial Park

Rocky Mtn House

Rocky Mountain House

12

53 Rimbey

Bentley

C

Strachan

Eckville

11

Sylvan Lake

Sylvan Lake

Dovercourt

Ricinus

Cheddarville

Crammond

54

Marketville

Dickson

20

3252m
Limestone Mtn

Gleniffer Park

James River Bridge

22

Innisfail

D

3373m
Willingdon

734

Bearberry

Sundre

27

Olds

Banff National Park

2962m
Barrier Mtn

Red Deer

2A

3373m

Didsbury

Moraine Lake

Cremona

2

Castle Junction

3162m
Mt Aylmer

Water Valley

Vermillion Pass
640m

Minnewanka Lake

Bow

Waiparous

Rosebud

72

Banff

Ghost Lake

Bow

Airdrie

Canmore

Exshaw

1A

Cochrane

22

Big Hill Spring

E

Vermilion Crossing

Kananaskis Country

Mount Assiniboine Park

CALGARY

8

3618m
Mt Assiniboine

6

Waterton Lakes National Park

7

8

F

141

Vancouver

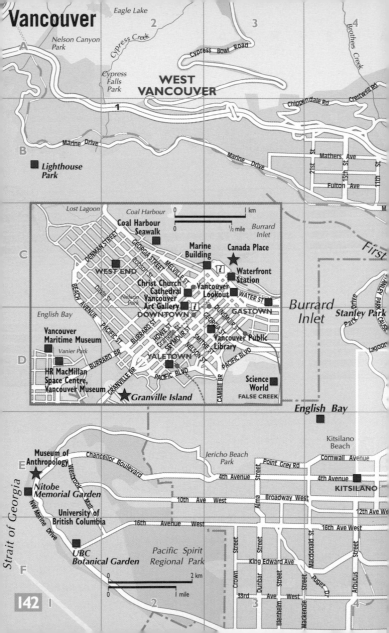

Eagle Lake

Nelson Canyon
Park

Cypress Creek

**WEST
VANCOUVER**

Cypress
Falls
Park

Cypress Bowl Road

Chippendale Rd

Crestwell Rd

Brothers Creek

Marine Drive

Marine Drive

21st St

Mathers Ave

15th St

11th St

Fulton Ave

■ Lighthouse
Park

Lost Lagoon

Coal Harbour

0   1 km

0   ½ mile

Burrard
Inlet

■ Coal Harbour
Seawalk

■ Marine
Building

★ Canada Place

PENMAN STREET

GEORGIA STREET

MELVILLE ST

ROBSON ST

i

■ Waterfront
Station

WEST END

■

Nelson Park

Christ Church
Cathedral

Vancouver
Lookout

WATER ST

i

■ Vancouver
Art Gallery

DOWNTOWN

HORNBY ST

GEORGIA ST

GASTOWN

■ Vancouver Public
Library

First

English Bay

BEACH AVENUE

PACIFIC ST

BURRARD ST

HOWE ST

GRANVILLE ST

SEYMOUR ST

SMITHE ST

NELSON ST

**Burrard
Inlet**

Stanley Park

STANLEY PARK CSWY

Park Drive

Lagoon

■ Vancouver
Maritime Museum

Vanier Park

DRIVE

BURRARD BR

GRANVILLE BR

YALETOWN

PACIFIC BLVD

CAMBIE BR

PACIFIC BLVD

■ HR MacMillan
Space Centre,
Vancouver Museum

★ Granville Island

■ Science
World

FALSE CREEK

■ English Bay

Kitsilano
Beach

■ Museum of
Anthropology

Chancellor Boulevard

Jericho Beach
Park

Point Grey Rd

Cornwall Avenue

★

Westbrook Mall

4th Avenue

Alma
Street

4th Avenue ■

KITSILANO

*Nitobe
Memorial Garden*

NW Marine Drive

10th Ave West

Broadway West

12th Ave W

Strait of Georgia

**University of
British Columbia**

16th   Avenue   West

16th Ave West

■ UBC
Botanical Garden

*Pacific Spirit
Regional Park*

Crown
Street

Dunbar
Street

King Edward Ave

Macdonald St

Puget Dr

Arbutus
Street

0   2 km

0   1 mile

33rd   Ave   West

Blenheim
St

Mackenzie
Street

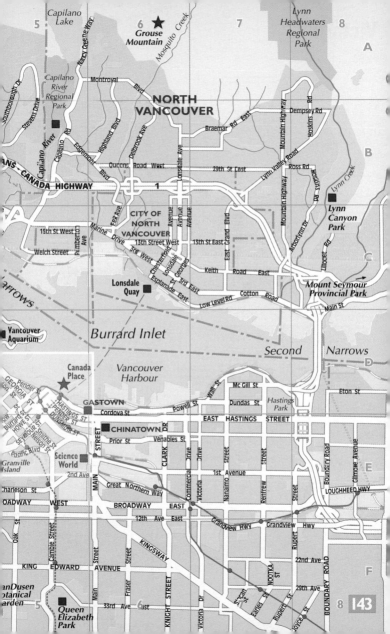

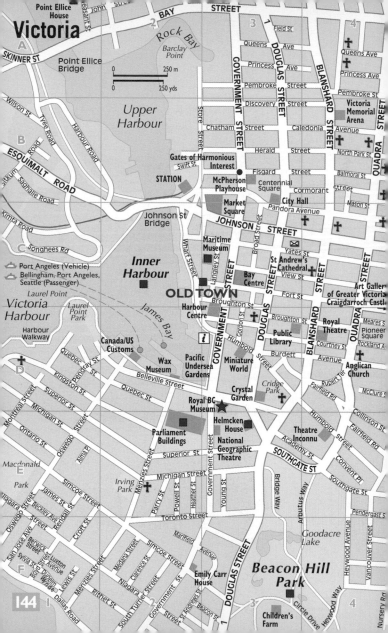

Victoria

A

Point Ellice House

BAY STREET

Rock Bay

Barclay Point

SKINNER ST

Point Ellice Bridge

Pleasant St John
Field St
3 1
4

Queens Ave

DOUGLAS STREET

Princess Ave

Queens Ave

Pembroke Street

GOVERNMENT STREET

Princess Ave

Victoria Memorial Arena

BLANSHARD STREET

Pembroke St

Discovery Street

250 m
0
250 yds

Chatham Street

Caledonia Avenue

B

Wilson St

Harbour Road

Tyee Road

ESQUIMALT ROAD

Sumac Road

Kimta Road

Songhees Rd

Saghalie Road

Herald Street

North Park St

QUADRA STREET

Fisgard Street

Balmoral St

Gates of Harmonious Interest

Swift St

STATION

McPherson Playhouse

Centennial Square

Mason St

Cormorant Street

Market Square

City Hall

Pandora Avenue

Johnson St Bridge

JOHNSON STREET

Upper Harbour

Store Street

C

Port Angeles (Vehicle)

Bellingham, Port Angeles, Seattle (Passenger)

Laurel Point

Johnson Street

Inner Harbour

Wharf Street

Maritime Museum

Langley Street

Broad Street

Yates St

St Andrew's Cathedral

View St

QUADRA STREET

Bay Centre

Fort St

Art Gallery of Greater Victoria

Craigdarroch Castle

OLD TOWN

Broughton St

D

Victoria Harbour

Laurel Point Park

Harbour Walkway

Quebec Street

Kingston St

Pendray St

Superior St

Canada/US Customs

James Bay

Harbour Centre

Wax Museum

Belleville Street

Quebec Street

i

Pacific Undersea Gardens

Miniature World

Crystal Garden

GOVERNMENT STREET

Gordon St

Humboldt St

DOUGLAS STREET

Broughton St

Public Library

Burdett

Cridge Park

Courtney St

BLANSHARD STREET

Royal Theatre

Pioneer Square

Meares St

Rockland Av

Anglican Church

Rupert Ter

Fairfield Rd

McClure

E

Montreal St

Ontario St

Michigan St

Oswego St

Alma St

Simcoe Street

Irving Park

Royal BC Museum

Parliament Buildings

Menzies Street

Powell St

Heather St

Government Street

National Geographic Theatre

Superior St

Helmcken House

Michigan Street

Young St

Academy St

Theatre Inconnu

Bridge Way

Southgate St

SOUTHGATE ST

Collinson St

Fairfield Rd

Humboldt Street

Convent Pl

Arbutus Way

Pendergast St

F

Macdonald Park

James St

Niagara St

Oswego St

Beckley Ave

Kendall St

Croft St

Simcoe Street

Parry St

Toronto Street

Medana St

Clarence St

Rithet St

Niagara St

Government Street

Emily Carr House

Marifield Avenue

Beacon Hill Park

Goodacre Lake

Heywood Avenue

Vancouver St

Circle Drive

Children's Farm

2
3
4

144